MODERATING
FOCUS
GROUPS

Thomas L. Greenbaum

MODERATING FOCUS GROUPS

A Practical

Guide for

Group

Facilitation

Sage Publications, Inc.
International Educational and Professional Publisher
Thousand Oaks ▪ London ▪ New Delhi

For information:

 Sage Publications, Inc.
2455 Teller Road
Thousand Oaks, California 91320
E-mail: order@sagepub.com

Sage Publications Ltd.
6 Bonhill Street
London EC2A 4PU
United Kingdom

Sage Publications India Pvt. Ltd.
M-32 Market
Greater Kailash I
New Delhi 110 048 India

Printed in the United States of America

Library of Congress Cataloging-in-Publication Data

Greenbaum, Thomas L.
  Moderating focus groups: A practical guide for group facilitation /
by Thomas L. Greenbaum.
        p.   cm.
  Includes index.
  ISBN 0-7619-2043-9 (cloth: alk. paper)
  ISBN 0-7619-2044-7 (pbk.: alk. paper)
1. Focused group interviewing.   2. Social sciences—Research.
I. Title.
  H61.28.G73   2000
  001.4'33—dc21   99-006959

This book is printed on acid-free paper.

           02   03   04   05   06   7   6   5   4   3   2

Acquisition Editor:	Harry Briggs
Editorial Assistant:	Mary Ann Vail
Production Editor:	Sanford Robinson
Editorial Assistant:	Cindy Bear
Typesetter:	Janelle LeMaster
Indexer:	Jeanne R. Busemeyer
Cover Designer:	Candice Harman

To Rosalie Montag Greenbaum
My Wife, Best Friend, and Favorite Person
Life With You Has Been a Wonderful Trip . . .
I Look Forward to the Next 30 Years!
and
To My Brother Allie . . .
Having You Back in the East
After All These Years
Means More Than You Will Ever Know.

CONTENTS

PREFACE

After completing a comprehensive revision of *The Handbook for Focus Group Research*, I promised myself this would be my last literary endeavor. It was my fourth book, and the third about focus groups (the other was about the consulting business), and I could not imagine identifying enough new material to warrant another revision of the *Handbook*. Beyond that, it seemed that I had said all I could about the profession to which I have dedicated the past 5 years of my working life. However, as I have continued to lecture at graduate schools of business, speak at conferences, and write for various magazines, I have come to realize that there is more information about focus groups to be shared with the profession.

As a result of the contacts I have made through my most recent book, my magazine writing, and the lecturing I have done, it has come to my attention that there has been an increase in inquiries from prospective, new, or even established moderators who want to improve their overall skills as a facilitator of focus groups. Though I have been aware for some time that there are formal courses offered by different organizations to train people to be moderators, the feedback I have received from people who have attended them has not been particularly positive, so I feel there is a real gap between what is available and what people are seeking. Perhaps the courses were good and the students bad, but it was clear to me that these courses were not achieving the objectives that at least some of the participants had for the instruction.

When I first considered the idea of writing a book on moderating, my initial reaction was that there was not enough material to fill an entire text. Further, I had always felt that moderating focus groups, or any other type of meeting, was something one learned by doing and that it would be extremely difficult to reduce the principles to writing and to create a meaningful text on the topic. Despite this initial reaction, I began to analyze the moderator's role in the qualitative research process, focusing mostly on the focus group methodology because of my personal bias toward that technique. The more I began to dissect this function, the better I began to feel about the possibility of a book. As a result of this analysis, I convinced myself that a great deal could be communicated to a target audience about moderating focus groups that would be useful to almost anyone in the field or others who were considering this as a career.

The text that follows is a result of this analysis. I hope you will find it to be a helpful guide that will provide the type of information that will make you a better moderator. As I discuss in later chapters of this book, the moderator of the future is someone who will be expected to be a highly competent facilitator but also to offer his or her clients more than simply moderation skills. Perhaps this book will help you to achieve your personal goals as a focus group moderator. I would be very receptive to any feedback about this book, and I encourage you to communicate to me through my Web site (www.groupsplus.com).

ACKNOWLEDGMENTS

M any people have been helpful to me in the development of this book. First and foremost are all the people in the marketing and research industry who have called and e-mailed me to ask about moderator training, as this was my main impetus for writing this book. I hope that it is helpful to all these people.

I want to express special thanks to my colleague Ella Kelley for all the help she provided to the book from the time I originally worked on the outline to the completion of the final manuscript. Her ideas were always helpful, insightful, and instructive and have resulted in a much more effective book than I would have created without her assistance. She is a very special person, and I am honored to have worked with her for the past 4 years.

Also I want to acknowledge the contribution of Elaine Shepherd, with whom I have worked closely for 26 years. We have grown old together (although she won't admit to the "old" part), and I have always appreciated the help she has provided, whether working on business or nonbusiness matters. She has typed every word of the five books I have written and is as much a part of these projects as I. For this I am truly appreciative.

I want to pay a very special tribute to Shelly Parker, who has worked with me as my field director over the past 8 years. She has been helpful to me in many different aspects of this book, including reviewing chapters that were particularly germane to her area of expertise, in addition to giving me the benefit of her very quick mind on various topics in the book about which I was seeking another point of view. I have been blessed with Shelly as a colleague these past years, and I appreciate the contribution she has made to the success of Groups Plus.

Finally, I want to thank some very special people at various client companies for whom I have worked in recent years. I am sure you know who you are and appreciate why I cannot recognize you individually. However, I feel that we at Groups Plus have been extremely lucky to have had such wonderful clients over the years, as they have made our work interesting, stimulating, fun, and even somewhat profitable. To all of you, I must say thanks!

1

INTRODUCTION

This book is written for people who facilitate discussions, including focus groups, individual in-depth interviews, or general business meetings. The principles of moderating are the same, whether the objective of the session is to conduct research or to share information among colleagues. I have chosen to write this book because I have been unable to uncover another text that gives current or prospective moderators sufficient practical, "how-to" information to be helpful to their success in the field of qualitative research.

When I began moderating focus groups many years ago, the only resources I had to learn from were other moderators, some of whom were effective and others of whom were not especially talented. As a product manager converting to the focus group industry, I took a long time to identify which practices of the various moderators that I observed could teach me something useful for entry into this field. It took me almost 5 years of moderating, or close to 500 groups, to develop and refine an approach to this profession that was effective and could provide a meaningful added value to my clients.

Unfortunately, however, most people who rely on focus group research have great difficulty telling the difference between a good and a bad moderator because several tangential factors can affect the perception of the moderator's skills. Clients' attitudes at the conclusion of a focus group project are often heavily influenced by the reaction of the participants to the topics being discussed or by the entertainment the clients got from observing the group, rather than by the validity of the findings or the depth of information that was obtained. Further, because focus groups are only one part of the overall marketing mix, the success or failure of a product or an idea is ultimately determined by many factors that are never even addressed in focus groups, so it is difficult for a client organization to look back on a project and reflect on the impact that the qualitative research had on the success or failure of the venture. Although this book is intended for moderators, I hope that many people who hire moderators to facilitate their sessions will review it, as it might provide them with some excellent insights on how to evaluate the moderators with whom they work and how to establish criteria for selecting those they hire.

A NOTE ABOUT A PERSONAL
BIAS IN THIS BOOK!

This book has been written to help anyone do a more effective job of facilitating a meeting. However, the bulk of the text will address moderating focus groups. Although this is only one form of moderating, it is the most popular type of marketing research used in America (and perhaps the world) today and therefore deserves the single-minded attention of a manual such as this book. Further, the focus group moderator is one of the few people in business who is consistently evaluated not just on the outcome of his or her work but on the manner in which information is obtained. Because they work in front of a one-way mirror almost 100% of the time, constantly being observed by superiors, peers, and clients, moderators need to pursue ways to maximize their technique and approach, acknowledging that the pressure to "perform" is always very great. Many moderators consider each day to be somewhat like the opening of a new show in which they perform and then are reviewed by the critics (superiors or clients) on the basis of the quality of their work.

My decision not to spend significant time addressing other types of facilitation in this book is not intended to suggest that they are not as challenging, difficult, or important as moderating focus groups. Rather, it is a recognition that I can do a much better job for the reader by concentrating my efforts on focus groups, confident that people will be able to take the principles outlined for the focus group technique and apply them to other types of facilitation. I have done this in my career, and I find that good facilitation skills are essentially the same whether one is conducting an individual interview, a focus group, a teleconference, or a business meeting.

WHAT ARE FOCUS GROUPS?

Focus groups are groups of 7 to 10 people, recruited on the basis of similar demographics, psychographics, buying attitudes, or behavior, who engage in a discussion, led by a trained moderator, of a particular topic. Thus, use of focus groups is a qualitative research technique. Its goal is to delve into attitudes and feelings about a particular topic, to understand the "why" behind the consumer behavior. The intent of using the group for the discussion is to encourage the participants in the session to interact with each other so that the quality of the output is enhanced. Some professionals in the qualitative research industry prefer to work with a mini-group, which is a focus group conducted among 4 to 6 people. Other than the absolute numbers of participants in the sessions, there are no substantive differences between mini-groups and full groups.

A focus group is normally conducted in a specially constructed facility that includes a discussion room and a client observation area, with the two places separated by a one-way mirror so that the people watching the session will not be seen by the participants. Although the ethics of focus groups requires the moderator to tell the participants that observers are watching the session, normally the identity of the people behind the mirror is not revealed. As will be discussed later in this book, if the moderator introduces the one-way mirror correctly, the participants will soon forget about the observers and essentially ignore the existence of the mirror.

For a discussion to be classified as a legitimate focus group, it should contain virtually all of the following characteristics:

- Be held in a facility where a one-way mirror exists to permit observers to watch the session
- Be conducted by an objective, external, trained facilitator
- Be composed of 7 to 10 people (or 4 to 6 for mini-groups) who were recruited on the basis of common characteristics
- Be implemented using a discussion guide that has been prepared in advance to ensure that the appropriate topics are covered in the session and that the proper amount of time is allocated to each
- Be executed in such a way that the participants interact with each other both verbally and nonverbally
- Contain a vehicle for the observers to communicate with the moderator during the session to ensure that the process is interactive between both parties
- Be conducted in an environment that is conducive to all participants' giving their complete attention to the discussion topics for the entire session

Many different types of discussions are inaccurately called *focus groups* because the basic technique has become so important to the overall research process that the moniker has been attached to many different types of interactions and information-gathering sessions that are *not* focus groups. For example:

- Internet chat sessions are often called *Internet focus groups* in an effort to try and benefit from the halo effect of the original tried and proven methodology. However, anyone who is a student of the focus group technique realizes that most of the elements that make the methodology successful (discussed in detail in Chapter 2) are not present in Internet chat sessions. Therefore, it is incorrect to call this type of research a focus group.
- Some organizations conduct telephone conferences and call them *telephone focus groups*. While this might be a viable means of collecting information, it is difficult to consider such conferences focus

groups for the same reasons that Internet sessions are not focus groups. Most of the basic elements that are integral to the focus group methodology are not present with the telephone research approach.

- Companies sometimes recruit people to a discussion as a way to expose them to a product in what is really a promotional session disguised as a focus group. For example, drug companies frequently recruit physicians to a central location under the guise of participating in a focus group, but the real intent of these meetings is to promote a new pharmaceutical product or service. Although these sessions often involve some discussion, they clearly are not intended to be research, and the structure and dynamics of the meetings do not conform to the basic characteristics of a focus group.

- Also, many people conduct internal business meetings (among employees or customers) and call them focus groups, with the objective of emphasizing the importance of encouraging discussion and interaction among the participants. However, these also should not be called focus groups because they do not contain the most fundamental elements that are required for a session to be considered a focus group.

FOCUS GROUPS AND THEIR ROLE
IN THE OVERALL MARKETING MIX

Focus groups are typically used in the early stages of product or concept development, when organizations are trying to create an overall direction for a marketing initiative. Because it is possible to change the content of focus groups from session to session, the dynamic nature of this technique makes it an excellent vehicle to explore ideas with consumers and then to modify them on the basis of what is learned from the sessions.

Whereas focus groups used to be considered only as a precursor to quantitative research (in which projectable numerical data are developed), in recent years the technique has been employed to give executives qualitative information that they can use in the decision-making process without necessarily doing quantitative research as a follow-up technique. With increasing pressure on companies to develop new products, advertising, or promotion on a faster timetable and with reduced research budgets, the tendency to use quantitative research following focus groups has declined significantly. As a result, the role of focus groups in the overall marketing process has changed from a purely exploratory technique to one that often represents the voice of the consumer on the future of a product, service, advertisement, or packaging innovation. This has placed new requirements on the focus group moderator in terms of bringing client organizations additional skills in drawing conclusions and understanding the marketing impact of research findings.

WHEN ARE FOCUS GROUPS APPROPRIATE, AND WHEN SHOULD THEY NOT BE USED?

As a general rule, focus groups are an appropriate research vehicle when the goal of the investigation is to gain an understanding of the "why" behind a consumer attitude or behavior. The strength of the focus group technique is that it enables a group of individuals to share their views in a nonthreatening environment, with the goal of learning about the factors that dictate a particular action or attitude. Because of the quick turnaround time and accessibility of focus groups, many marketing professionals seeking information today immediately look to focus groups as a way to get answers to their questions. The first four words in my first book on focus groups were "Let's do some groups"—a suggestion that reflects the attitudes of many people who are faced with the need to find information. But although focus groups can be a very effective part of a research program, this technique is not always the most appropriate way to gather information, and in some situations the output may be more misleading than helpful. Therefore, it is important to understand when focus groups are and are not appropriate so that the methodology can be applied to the situations in which the technique will provide the greatest return.

It is probably easiest to address this question by first asking when focus groups are *not* an appropriate research vehicle and when it would be prudent to employ a different qualitative or quantitative technique. Focus groups are not appropriate

- When the goal of the research is to be able to develop quantitative outputs that the user plans to incorporate into a projection, such as a sales estimate or a pricing model. The qualitative research methodology is not oriented toward generating numerical outputs, although some users do try to project sales, advertising recall, or the trial-generating impact of a promotion on the basis of reactions from focus groups.

- When the goal of the research is to obtain consumer inputs regarding the selection of different product formulations or packaging graphics. Although focus groups are often used for this purpose, the outputs must be considered qualitative because of the methodology and nonprojectable sample size. Normally, product and package preference testing requires a quantitative methodology so that statistical significance testing can be employed to provide a basis for the validity of the outputs.

- When the topic material being covered could not be addressed objectively by the participants. For example, if the criteria for recruiting the participants requires that the individuals be competitors, the dynamics of focus groups will not work: These people generally will not provide honest, objective inputs because of the need for confidentiality and security regarding their corporate interests.

- When the participants required for a group are widely dispersed geographically and cannot be economically brought together in the same room. This is often the case when groups are conducted among very specialized market segments, where the universe of candidates is small and candidates are not located in the same geographic area. In this case, individual interviews, dyads, or triads would be a much more appropriate research technique.

Some people believe that the focus group methodology is not appropriate for use with very sensitive personal topics, such as those relating to health, sex, money, or religion. However, it has been my experience that if the sensitive topic is handled professionally by the moderator, most people will actually be more comfortable talking about it in a group than in a one-to-one environment. In a later chapter, we will address the controversy in the industry regarding the use of focus groups versus individual in-depth interviews as the most effective methodology for generating qualitative research information.

2

THE FOCUS GROUP METHODOLOGY

Why the Technique Works So Effectively

Focus groups have served as an effective research method for almost 50 years, with dramatically increased usage during the last decade of the 20th century, suggesting that focus groups will continue to be used well into the next millennium. An understanding of the key factors that make focus groups work provides the basis for identifying appropriate opportunities for the technique and for recognizing the key differences between focus groups and the other competing methodologies (one-on-ones, Internet chats, telephone groups, etc.).

THE ELEMENTS THAT MAKE FOCUS GROUPS WORK

As a student of the focus group methodology over the past 20 years, I have identified several different elements that I believe are integral to

9

the technique and contribute to the effectiveness of this methodology as a universally accepted research approach.

The Authority of the Moderator

The authoritarian role of the moderator in the process is vital to the success of the technique, as this individual is the designated leader of the session. In this role, the moderator is vested with the authority to direct the participants in the group to follow his or her instructions regarding the topic areas being discussed and to ensure the involvement of the participants in the discussion of those areas. If the authority role of the moderator is questioned by the participants (as will be discussed in a later chapter), the overall efficacy of the group can be seriously affected. A moderator who cannot control a group discussion will be unable to ensure the quality of the group's output.

The Ability to Use Both Verbal and Nonverbal Inputs as Part of the Learning Process

Because the focus group process uses face-to-face interactions of a group as the essential output vehicle, both the moderator and the participants can react to the others in the room on the basis of both verbal and nonverbal communications. An experienced moderator will often pursue nonverbal signs from a participant, addressing specific questions to the participant or probing an area more with this individual on the basis of a combination of verbal and nonverbal commentary. Focus groups are the only research technique in which even unintended reactions from participants can be used to delve further into a particular topic of interest.

The Group Dynamics in the Room

One of the most important reasons to use focus group research is to benefit from the interactions of the participants in the room. An effective focus group moderator will work hard to encourage group discussion so that the opinions of one participant can be shared with the others and then will hopefully evoke some reactions and interactions. The effective use of group dynamics enables a moderator to encourage those people in the room who share one point of view to try to convince those who have the opposing perspective, and vice versa. As a result of this process, the richness of the information generated in the session can be dramatically improved as each side draws on more reasons for its view. Further, with this type of interaction among the participants, issues will often emerge from the discussion that would normally not evolve if the moderator was asking opinions of each of the participants in a one-on-one format without encouraging the group interaction.

The Concentrated Attention of the Participants

In a focus group environment, the participants know in advance that they are expected to be involved in the session for approximately 2 hours. During this time, the participants are sitting in a room with the moderator and do not have the opportunity to do anything other than be engaged in the group process, participating in the discussion when appropriate. As a result, their attention is directed to the topic area for the full length of the group session. This is in contrast with some other qualitative techniques such as Internet chats or telephone groups, in which there is no way to know what participants might be doing while "involved" in the session. For example, they could be watching television, reading a book or magazine, or working on a spreadsheet and as a result not devoting their complete attention to the topic areas under discussion on the telephone or the computer screen.

The Ability of Client Personnel to Be Directly Involved in the Research Process

One of the most important strengths of the focus group process is the ability of clients to watch the research live. This enables the client to actually see the research in process, participate in ongoing decisions and modifications, and understand fully the dynamics of the participants. This enhances the credibility of the conclusions at the end of the project and fosters a cooperative and constructive approach to results. In quantitative research and in many different types of qualitative studies, it is not possible for clients to watch the entire research, so they rely on the judgment of the moderator, the impressions of their own personnel, or the data from a quantitative study based on respondent interviews. We have consistently found that our clients accept research findings more positively when the key executives who will make decisions based on the research have been observers of the groups.

Safety in Numbers

One of the strong elements of the focus group technique is the security that people feel when talking about sensitive topics with others who are similarly affected. Some people in the research industry feel that very personal subjects are better handled using a one-on-one methodology, but I have found that it is both possible and extremely effective to cover these types of subjects in a group. For example, I have successfully conducted focus groups with both men and women about incontinence and about toilet tissue, have talked with women whose spouse died in the last 6 months, and talked with women about vaginal warts. These are very difficult topics to cover, but when they are addressed appropriately in a professional manner, the participants are able to get past the potential embarrassment and provide useful inputs on them.

Controls Over Security

One of my favorite cartoons from the *New Yorker* magazine showed two dogs sitting in front of a computer. One said to the other, "On the Internet, nobody knows we are dogs." This is one of the many reasons why traditional focus groups are a more effective technique than Internet or telephone focus groups. With the proper screening and rescreening of participants, there is no question who is involved in the discussion, and we know that there are no uninvited guests listening in on the session. In an era where security is so important to the marketing research process, I find it comforting to know that we have some control over who really is involved in our focus groups and are assured that no outsiders are being exposed to the inputs.

The Dynamic Nature of the Process

A major advantage of focus groups (and many other qualitative methodologies) over quantitative research is the dynamic nature of the process. Because each focus group session is actually an individual research project in itself, it is possible to change the research from group to group in order to benefit from the learning of the early sessions and improve the quality of the output in the later ones. An example of this might be the exposure of a new product concept to a target audience. What is learned from the first group or two might suggest some problems with the way the concept statement was written or the emphasis that was placed on the various product features and benefits. This learning can provide the stimulus for a modification in the concept statement so that subsequent groups are exposed to a different version that is more reflective of the interests of consumers.

Another example of a crucial midcourse correction unique to this type of research involves the recruitment of group participants. One major company that was offering a new computer capability felt that it would need to explore the attitudes of a group of departmental executives because they were an integral part of the overall purchase decision process for this type of equipment. The company assumed that the executives would confer with the information technology (IT) specialists and jointly make decisions regarding the hardware needed to meet the stated objectives. But after the first few groups, it was evident that the departmental executives might tell the IT specialists requirements related to the output of the management information system but that they were not at all involved in any discussions on hardware. The result of this was a change in the definition of the target participant, and the groups conducted in the later part of the program were able to generate the type of information that could achieve the objectives of the study.

The Speed of the Process

Today's research environment is one of rapid response, with many companies demanding research findings almost immediately. Many organizations are not willing to wait 10 to 14 weeks to conduct a quantitative study for fear that the marketplace will have passed them by when the results are finally available. With qualitative research, and focus groups specifically, it is possible to generate a significant amount of very useful research information in a 2- to 4-week period. Most focus group projects can be implemented within 4 weeks from the time that approval is received to proceed with the study. This is one of the most important factors that has contributed to the growth of focus groups in recent years.

The Absolute Cost of the Research

Another major reason that the focus group technique works in the current business environment is its relatively low cost as compared to the cost of most quantitative research studies. For example, it is possible to conduct a very small (two-group) study for under $10,000, which makes this type of research affordable to small companies or to others who want to do some preliminary exploratory research without committing significant sums of money to the process. Although the cost per participant in focus groups is dramatically higher than would be realized in a quantitative study, the absolute dollar outlay is generally much less. This is very appealing to organizations seeking to minimize the expenditures for market research.

In summary, focus groups continue to gain appeal as a research tool because they offer clients a flexible, fast, and cost-effective way to gain insight into consumer attitudes, behavior, and needs. As a vibrant, interactive means of probing a variety of issues, focus groups offer clients ongoing access to information on their products and services, including consumer reactions to hypotheses that are derived from the group input.

3

FOCUS GROUPS VERSUS ONE-ON-ONE (IN-DEPTH) INTERVIEWS

Over the past 20 years, one of the most controversial topics I have been asked to address on a regular basis is whether a research effort should use focus groups or the one-on-one interview methodology, also known as in-depth interviews or IDIs. My experience has been that most people in the research community have strong feelings about this topic and are either very much in favor of using focus groups or believe that the best way to gather qualitative data is via one-on-ones. There also are some who prefer mini-groups to full groups, believing that a moderator will get more out of a few people over a 2-hour period than he or she would from a full group of 8 to 10 people. We will not address the question of full versus mini-groups in this text, as it is a subjective area and I really do not believe there are strong arguments in favor of either alternative.

AN OVERVIEW OF IDIs

The basic premise of the individual in-depth interview is that a discussion is conducted between a participant and a facilitator about a particular topic of interest to the sponsoring organization. Normally, IDIs are conducted using a discussion guide much like one that would be employed in focus group research, although some interviewers are much more casual about one-on-ones and therefore conduct the discussion with only informal notes.

The length of individual in-depth interviews varies from very short (i.e., 15 to 20 minutes) to extremely long (i.e., 2 or more hours), depending on the needs of the research and the technique of the moderator. Generally, the very short interviews are conducted to obtain inputs from participants about specific issues of very limited scope, such as the communication message in one advertising execution or the image conveyed by one logo or package design. The longer interviews tend to focus more on attitudes and behaviors of individuals related to much more complex subjects, which require extensive warm-up discussion and in-depth probing to gather the information that is desired.

Unlike focus groups, which are almost always conducted in a specially constructed facility with a one-way mirror, individual in-depth interviews are conducted in many different venues. Most sponsors prefer using a special facility with a one-way mirror, like a focus group room, except that the interviewing area is much smaller. The benefit of this approach is that client personnel can observe the sessions and therefore be involved in the research effort so that modifications in approach or content can be built into the process to maximize the output.

One-on-one interviews are also frequently conducted outside traditional one-way mirror facilities, as it is often much easier and less expensive to hold the sessions in a participant's office, in a neutral location such as a hotel room, or even on the telephone. The principal disadvantages of these venues are that it is very difficult to include a client observer in the interview (without being dishonest as to the identity of the individual) and, in the case of telephone research, that you lose the benefit of face-to-face contact with the person. Also, when interviews are conducted in a client's office, it is sometimes difficult to avoid disruptions from telephone calls or visitors, which can diminish the ability of both the facilitator and the interviewee to maintain focus on the topic.

THE ARGUMENT FOR ONE-ON-ONES

The practitioners who prefer one-on-ones to focus groups tend to be working in the advertising agency business or as independent moderators who rely on the advertising agency industry for a great deal of their revenues. As a result, it has been our experience that one-on-ones are used more to help organizations evaluate consumer reactions to advertising copy than for any other purpose. The primary benefits of using one-on-ones instead of focus groups are considered to be:

- *The format offers the researcher the ability to probe more in depth with the participant.* People who use IDIs feel that they are able to get more substantive information than is possible with the focus group technique because of the greater concentration of time spent with each participant (normally 30 to 60 minutes) and the ability to use specialized probing techniques such as *laddering* to delve into the views of the individual. There is a feeling among users of one-on-ones that the increased time and focused attention with an individual will result in the development of attitudinal and behavioral insights into this person that would not be possible to obtain using focus groups.
- *People may be more willing to share more in an individual versus a group environment.* There is a very strong feeling among people who prefer one-on-ones that this technique is particularly effective because it eliminates the negative effects of group dynamics in which some participants are more interested in looking smart in the room with their peers or simply having a desire to communicate the "politically correct" views, rather than how they really feel. In addition, there is a belief that sensitive topics, such as those dealing with finances, personal hygiene, religion, or politics, can be addressed more effectively in an individual interview than a group situation. This is because of the embarrassment (or strong personal conviction) that is anticipated when a participant is asked to talk about these types of topics among a group of his or her peers.

- *The technique offers greater and more rapid flexibility in content covered.* In an earlier chapter, we talked about the importance of the dynamic nature of the focus group process in that the content can change from group to group on the basis of what is learned from the sessions. This argument for increased flexibility is important to the one-on-one technique because it is possible to change the content and direction of the research from interview to interview so that each subsequent session can build on the information generated in the previous interviews.

- *With IDIs, the researcher has access to a greater pool of moderators because the one-on-one technique is generally considered to be easier to conduct than group discussions.* This is because the one-on-one technique requires only that an individual be capable of facilitating a quality interview with one person and not that he or she develop the skills needed to control and facilitate discussion among 7 to 10 different people. Thus, it is very common for research companies to use more junior people to conduct one-on-one interviews than they would use for focus groups. The implications are that the total cost of the research can be reduced or that a greater number of interviews can be conducted at a lower cost.

- *It can be easier to analyze the output from one-on-one research than from focus groups.* This is because the listener/viewer has to assimilate the information from only one person rather than a group, so the task of understanding the key outputs from the session is much easier. Moreover, because the topics addressed in IDIs tend to be more narrow in scope, the analysis of the findings is often more straightforward.

THE CASE AGAINST ONE-ON-ONE RESEARCH

Many researchers routinely shy away from using one-on-one research for reasons that are outlined below. However, even for these researchers, there are some times when one-on-one research is an appropriate and preferred method of research. The following are the most common points raised concerning the limitations of the one-on-one research technique:

- *Individual interviews do not have the benefits of group dynamics that are integral to the overall effectiveness of the focus group technique.* For those moderators who are skilled in working with groups and encouraging the participants to share their views with others in the room, the one-on-one technique is considered to be significantly lacking. By its very nature, this methodology does not provide any way for the person being interviewed to share ideas with a peer so that the two of them can build on or argue about a topic being discussed. The result can sometimes be an outcome that is less rich in detail and ideas.

- *There also is a feeling among many researchers that with one-on-one interviews, even when the facilitator gets a good deal of information, much of it may not be as valid or useful as that obtained from focus groups.* This is because in the one-on-one environment, when the interviewee is asked a question, there is the expectation that he or she will answer it because the discussion is only between two people. The pressure on the interviewee to come up with an answer is further increased by the focus of the moderator, which is to try and delve as deeply into the feelings of the participant as possible to understand the real reasons for the participant's attitudes or behavior. However, this expectation for a response can put an invalid burden on the respondent, who may not have a point of view about a topic being discussed and should therefore have the option not to offer his or her views on the topic. In the focus group methodology, a trained moderator will know the difference between a participant who is shy or just reluctant to talk and one who simply does not care or have a point of view about the topic being discussed. Therefore, it is possible to isolate that person from the discussion so that the moderator does not force a response to a topic area when any comments will be contrived and possibly misleading. In the one-on-one technique, this is much more difficult to accomplish, due to the combined desire of the interviewee to please the moderator by answering all the questions that are asked and the mission of the facilitator to probe into the mind of the participant at all costs. As a result, it is not uncommon in one-on-one interviews to obtain inputs from people that really do not reflect their personal commitment or their point of view but rather represent an effort to answer the question raised because the moderator expects a response.

- *The economic value of one-on-ones is less than that of other types of qualitative research.* This is based on the relative costs of one-on-one interviews compared to focus groups when like numbers of people are involved. For example, the total cost to conduct three one-on-ones is typically very similar to the cost of one focus group, yet there is a very significant difference in the absolute number of people who are involved in the research.

- *It is very difficult to obtain the same degree of client involvement in one-on-ones as in focus groups.* This is a function of both the absolute time commitment required for attending the full series of one-on-ones that are conducted and the boredom factor that seems to set in as a result of observing a series of interviews about the same topic.

- *Many moderators feel it is extremely difficult to stay fresh when facilitating a series of one-on-one interviews.* This is due primarily to the repetitive nature of the content and the difficulty remembering whether various subject areas have been covered in the current interview. The repetition stems from the narrow focus of the subject matter in one-on-ones and the relative predictability of the flow of the interviews when there is no group interaction. The resulting boredom factor can make it very difficult for the facilitator to maintain the enthusiastic, upbeat demeanor that is essential to implementing effective one-on-one interviews, where each respondent must be made to feel that his or her responses are new and critical to the issue under discussion.

- *A final point that is frequently raised about one-on-ones concerns the willingness of participants to talk about sensitive topics in an individual in-depth interview environment.* Some moderators believe this is a preferred venue, whereas others do believe in the "safety in numbers" that is generally attributed to the focus group technique. It is unlikely that proponents of each side of this issue will ever agree about which is preferred, but it is important to raise the subject as one of the perceived disadvantages of one-on-one interviews.

In summary, it is almost certain that both the focus group and one-on-one methodologies will continue to thrive because there are advantages to both and because individual clients or researchers will always have reasons to prefer one over the other. When deciding which technique to use, clients should work with the project moderator to weigh issues of cost, the number of interviews, and the value of group dynamics relative to dynamics of a private, direct forum in obtaining honest and complete information.

4

THE ROLE OF THE MODERATOR

This chapter will discuss the moderator's role as the facilitator of discussions and as the person responsible for managing the total research process to deliver groups that are successful. The content of this chapter applies equally to individuals who facilitate focus groups or one-on-one interviews because the basic principles relating to the moderator's role are the same for each.

The intent of this chapter is to provide the new or prospective moderator with an overview of the moderating profession in terms of the most important tasks that this person is expected to perform to be an effective facilitator.

THE ROLE OF THE MODERATOR

Any discussion of the role of the moderator in the qualitative research process must begin with a statement that because there is no accepted standard for what tasks a moderator should perform, the role of this individual is not fixed or predictable. Rather, it varies dramatically depending on the experience of the moderator, the type of organization within which the person is working, the nature of the client for whom the research is conducted, and the prior relationship of the moderator and the client organization. Some general parameters on these issues are discussed below.

The more experienced the moderator, the more control he or she is likely to exert over the entire research process, from initial conceptualization of the methodology through the completion and presentation of the final report.

Some sponsor organizations expect the moderators that they retain to accept complete responsibility for all aspects of the research project, whereas others want to retain control of almost all elements other than the actual moderation of the groups.

This section outlines the role of a moderator on the basis of the assumption that this individual will be in complete control of the process and involved in all aspects of the strategic planning, recruiting, moderation, and report development. Although many moderators will not fill all these roles, I consider it important to describe the most comprehensive role in order to provide the greatest amount of assistance to prospective focus group or IDI facilitators. Importantly, most sponsors of focus groups view the moderator as the person responsible for successfully completing the research initiative. If something goes wrong that affects the end result, it is normally the moderator who is assigned the blame. As a result, we feel it is essential that moderators have an in-depth understanding of all the possible roles that they could play so that even if they are not provided with responsibility for a particular element, they will be aware of what is happening with this phase of the study in order to minimize the chances that problems will occur.

The following will identify the various roles of a moderator in the overall focus group research process.

Strategic Consultant and Planner

Many client organizations or sponsors of qualitative research expect their moderator to provide assistance on the overall strategic components of the research process. These include at least the following areas:

1. Providing advice regarding the most appropriate research methodology that should be used to achieve the objectives of the study within the established budget. For example, although the client organization often will come to a moderator seeking help in implementing focus groups, at the same time they expect the moderator to advise them as to whether focus groups are the most appropriate methodology, or whether another qualitative (or quantitative) approach would achieve the goals of the research more effectively.

2. Assisting the client organization in developing clear-cut objectives for the research so that the study can be properly constructed and the results evaluated in light of the goals that were established. An experienced moderator will insist that the objectives of the research be committed to writing and approved by all concerned, so that there will be no questions later on in the process about what the client was trying to achieve with the research.

3. Helping the client determine the specifications of the research including such key elements as

   The number of groups to be conducted
   The geographic locations where the sessions are to be held
   The specifications of the participants so that the right people are recruited for the groups
   The "external stimuli" that will need to be created to maximize the value of the output from the groups. Chapter 10 provides a detailed discussion of external stimuli and how they are integral to the focus group research process.

4. Providing help to the client contact personnel regarding the most effective way to communicate the results of the research to senior management so that the output from the research achieves maximum results.

Content Manager

Although most clients normally come to moderators with a reasonable understanding of what they are trying to learn in focus groups, they do rely on the moderator to develop a comprehensive discussion guide that outlines the topics to be covered in the session and the timing that will be associated with each. Chapter 9 contains a detailed discussion of the moderator guide in terms of how it is developed, what it contains, and how the moderator uses it with the client and the participants.

In addition to the development of the discussion guide, focus group moderators are often called on to assist in the development of the external stimuli for the groups, whether they are concept statements, a series of one-liners, or an advertising or packaging presentation. The moderator is expected to be able to provide guidance to the client organization on the most appropriate external stimuli in light of the objectives of the research, and often on how this material is to be written so that it works most effectively to achieve the objectives of the groups.

Project Coordinator/Implementer

In addition to the role as strategy and content consultant, the focus group moderator is generally charged with responsibility of making the groups happen in the field. This element of the job includes the following specific segments:

- Selection of the most appropriate focus group facility in the markets that were selected for the study. Choosing the right facility involves considering such things as the geographic location of the local research company vis-à-vis the anticipated location of the prospects, the facility's experience in recruiting the types of people who are specified for the groups, and the facility's setup to handle the needs of the situation (i.e., large back-room viewing area, kitchen facilities, videoconferencing hookup, etc.). An in-depth discussion of the focus group facility and how to work most effectively with these organizations is contained in Chapter 13 of my *Handbook for Focus Group Research.*
- Developing the recruiting screening questionnaire and managing the entire recruitment process to ensure that the right number of qualified participants come to the sessions. This subject is covered in great detail in Chapter 7 of this book.
- Coordinating the more mundane administrative details of the focus group process such as the times of the groups; the requirements in the group room for easels, VCRs, Internet connections, and so forth; food to be served to the client observers; and the process to be used by the facility to rescreen the participants to ensure that when

they arrive at the facility they meet the established criteria for participation.

Facilitator

The most obvious and critical role of the moderator is to facilitate the groups in such a way that the objectives of the research are accomplished. The client organization assumes that the moderator has the skills to implement the content of the discussion guide so that the desired information is obtained from the participants. This includes developing approaches to draw out people who are reluctant to participate in the groups, handling those who try to dominate the sessions, and ensuring a reasonably equitable distribution of discussion among all the participants in each of the groups.

An important implied role of the facilitator is the ability to use moderation techniques that will "peel away the onion" and delve into the real reasons for the attitudes or behaviors that are indicated. An integral part of this is to leverage the energy of the entire group to explore the topic areas in depth, while making sure that interpersonal dynamics of the group do not influence the views of the various members in a way that prevents them from communicating their true beliefs. It is essential that the moderator eliminate the kind of group pressure that can make some participants give responses that they feel will be most acceptable among their immediate group of peers.

Analyst and Communicator

Other than the role of actually moderating the groups, the most important contribution that a qualified moderator can make to a research program is to analyze the inputs from the participants in the groups and develop supportable conclusions and recommendations. Then the moderator must be able to develop the appropriate written and/or oral presentation of the findings, conclusions, and recommendations so that these will be easily understood by the necessary people in the client organization. Implied in this is the capability of the moderator to write the report in such a way that the recommendations will be accepted by the client organization and implemented as appropriate.

Psychologist/Friend

An effective moderator is also expected to be available to his or her clients when issues arise in the organization regarding the research and the client contact person needs help. This assistance could consist of providing suggestions to the contact person about the most effective way to sell the project to the people with control over the budget or simply helping the client contact people explain the approach used to conduct the research. It could also include assistance in resolving controversies relating to the objectives and scope of the research, the markets used, the number of groups proposed, or the specific type of stimulus material that will be used during the sessions to elicit responses from the participants.

In summary, the role of the moderator will always vary from one project to another depending upon a client organization's structure and needs, the experience of the moderator, and the nature of the research project. In all cases, the moderator will be responsible for managing the group discussions themselves, including content and control of the group dynamics. In addition, the role will often expand to include strategic consulting, project coordination, analysis, and client partnership. The best moderators are always prepared to fill all these functions.

5

THE CHARACTERISTICS OF A
SUCCESSFUL MODERATOR

According to a recent survey conducted by the Advertising Research Foundation, the average full-time focus group moderator conducts approximately 100 groups per year. Why is it that some moderators do more than 200 groups a year whereas others conduct significantly fewer than 100? The answer to this question probably can be obtained from an analysis of the key personal and professional characteristics that are associated with successful moderators.

The purpose of this chapter is to explore both the personal and the professional characteristics that we have found to be essential to success in the qualitative research industry. Though it is naive to think that one must have all the characteristics to achieve success (however that might be defined) in this industry, I do believe that the likelihood of building a good reputation and earning an acceptable living as a focus group moderator will increase dramatically if an individual can improve upon or, in some cases, acquire the characteristics addressed in this chapter.

PERSONAL CHARACTERISTICS

Over the past several years, I have known several people who have been very successful developing a focus group research business. It always interested me that these people all seemed to share some personal characteristics that I feel probably contributed to their success. For the most part, it is my observation that the personal characteristics that are necessary to be successful in this business are basic to the personality of the individuals, and one either has them or does not. Unlike the professional characteristics that are discussed in the next section of this chapter, it is almost impossible to develop the types of personal characteristics that are essential to an individual's success as a focus group moderator.

The following are those personal characteristics that I feel are most important to a person who seeks a successful career as a focus group moderator.

Hard Working

The nature of the focus group industry requires moderators to work very long hours, often under very stressful conditions. Because most focus groups are conducted in the evening (from 6 to 10 p.m.), the typical moderator will use the normal business day for business development, client relations, project implementation tasks, and report writing and then work in the evening to conduct the groups. As a result, it is not unusual for a successful moderator to work a 15-hour day 3 to 4 days a week, and then 8 to 10 hours on 2 other days.

Self-Motivating

Most moderators work as independent contractors unless they are working for an organization for which focus groups are only part of their job or unless they are entry-level researchers seeking to learn the skills so that they can build their own practice. Because there is generally no hierarchical structure in a focus group business, the individual must have the internal desire to be successful and be willing to make the sacrifices to achieve this goal. Importantly, this motivation must come from the individual: There are rarely others around who will provide positive reinforcement for the hard work, and most clients expect a high-quality research effort and therefore are not likely to dole out significant kudos for a job well done. The successful moderator should know when he or she has done a good job and be rewarded by the self-satisfaction obtained from realizing the excellent work that has been accomplished.

Self-Confident

The nature of the focus group moderator's position is that of a consultant, so client organizations expect their moderator to be professional and confident in his or her abilities. As a result, when asked for an opinion about a topic, the moderator must respond in such a way that both his or her demeanor and the content of the answer inspire the confidence of the client organization. If the moderator does not seem to have this confidence, the client may be more inclined to view him or her as a "vendor" of focus group services rather than a focus group research consultant.

Another element of self-confidence that is extremely important to successful moderators is the ability to work in an environment where they are observed by others when doing their work. As indicated in an earlier chapter of this book, focus group moderating is one of the few positions in the marketing community in which the individual is almost always watched by several others while doing his or her work. If a person is not confident in his or her abilities as a moderator, or exhibits reluctance to be observed when working in the profession, it is very unlikely that focus groups will be a viable career for him or her.

A Quick Learner, Able to Assimilate Large Amounts of (Often Complicated) Material Very Quickly

One of the most enjoyable aspects of the focus group industry is the variety of types of projects in which a moderator normally gets involved. For example, it would not be unusual for a moderator to work on a soft drink, a Web site, a health and beauty aid product, a computer, and a financial services project all in a period of a few weeks. In each case, the moderator is expected to learn enough about the various businesses or product categories so that he or she can develop an effective discussion guide and, during the group discussion, detect nuances that are important and ask appropriate follow-up questions. If an individual does not like the challenge of becoming an "instant expert" in a large number of different product and service categories, he or she will not be happy or successful as a focus group moderator.

Friendly, With the Ability to Develop a Quick Rapport With People

A moderator will get the most out of focus groups if the participants find him or her to be friendly and engaging, rather than aloof and disengaged. To this end, it is essential that a moderator be able to quickly develop this relationship with the participants, for the session lasts less than 2 hours, and it is vital to maximize the output from the group while they are in the room.

A Good Listener Who Is Comfortable Listening Rather Than Talking

The most effective focus group moderators do a relatively small amount of talking and a great deal of listening. The more a moderator can encourage the participants to talk, the richer the output from the groups is likely to be. Importantly, while the moderator is encouraging people to talk, he or she should concentrate on what they are saying. Further, a key element of the listening skills that an effective moderator must have is the ability to take in the substance of what the participants are saying and store it in his or her memory for use later in the groups. For example, it is often important to challenge a participant who seems to be offering one point of view early in the groups and another as the session proceeds. The output from this type of discussion can be extremely helpful in identifying the *real* feelings of individuals or in gaining an appreciation for which of the various stimuli presented during the group have changed their views from earlier in the session.

An Excellent Memory and Strong Powers of Concentration

One of the most important abilities of a successful moderator is the ability to remember what happens in the focus groups so that it is not necessary to regularly listen to the tapes in order to get the substance from the discussions. This skill takes a great deal of personal training but does seem to make a major difference in the overall quality of life and profitability of a focus group research business. For example, if a project involves 8 hours of groups (four sessions), the requirement to listen to all the tapes before writing the final report will add one working day to the overall time allocated to the assignment. The moderator will have to be willing either to charge for this time (which could price him or her out of the market) or to reduce the profitability on each assignment by a considerable amount due to the additional time needed to conduct the analysis and write the report.

Capable of Handling a Difficult Work Schedule

One of the biggest drawbacks of the moderating profession is the vast amount of travel that is required. Almost all focus group projects are conducted in more than one city, so it is necessary for the moderator to be willing to spend considerable amounts of time driving long distances or flying from market to market to conduct the sessions. Some people are not comfortable with this amount of travel because of either its impact on their physical being or their desire not to be away from home and family on a regular basis.

PROFESSIONAL CHARACTERISTICS

We have found several professional characteristics to be essential for a moderator to achieve success in the focus group research business. All of the characteristics discussed below can be learned if the moderator has the proper type of training and is willing to work hard to develop the skills that are identified.

Excellent Communication Skills

A successful focus group moderator is required to communicate with different constituency groups on a regular basis and in a variety of ways. For example:

- The moderator must be able to communicate orally to the focus group participants so that the questions asked or issues raised during the sessions are easily understood by the participants. Importantly, the moderator must be able to do this with many different types of participants, ranging from young children to teens, traditional working adults, and perhaps high-level business professionals, physicians, or other professionals.

- The moderator must be able to communicate the findings from the focus groups to the client organization in a written document. This is often the area that separates moderators, as some have developed excellent written and oral skills, whereas others have great difficulty expressing themselves clearly and concisely. The importance of effective written communications also is especially important because the focus group report is the representation of the work done by the moderator that most people in the client organization will see. Senior management in client organizations and others who are only peripherally involved in a project may not attend the groups, so their impression of the work conducted by the moderator is formed by the report to which they are exposed.

- It is also essential for a moderator to be comfortable with oral presentations in front of client personnel at all levels. Some clients ask for oral presentations of focus group results in addition to or instead of a written report, as it gives them an opportunity to interact directly with the moderator about the specific subject matter of the groups. If this presentation is not handled in a very professional manner, the impression the moderator gives to the client organization will not be favorable. There also is a need for moderators to provide brief oral presentations to the client personnel when using videoconferencing as a way to involve more client personnel in the focus group process. When this approach is employed in a focus groups series, it is generally necessary for the moderator to provide a summary presentation at the conclusion of each day's groups so that the people in the remote location(s) can benefit from the moderator's perspective at this point in the process.

Excellent Organizational Skills

A successful moderator will have many different things happening at the same time, all of which require effective management if the focus group process is to proceed smoothly. Because a large percentage of the people who operate as focus group moderators are sole practitioners, operating with no (or very limited) staff, the moderator must stay on top of all the details to ensure that nothing is omitted that could jeopardize the success of the project. This requires that an individual develop a system for keeping track of all the details involved in planning, implementing, and analyzing the focus group results and be able to stay on top of all of them for the duration of the project.

Another key reason that an effective focus group moderator should be extremely well organized is to be able to write the focus group reports while the material is fresh in his or her mind. Although a large percentage of moderators do not write their own reports (instead using project people to develop them from the tapes), those who do develop their own documents will find that it is dramatically easier to write a report within 3 days of the last group than if a substantial period of time has elapsed between the end of the research and the beginning of the writing process.

The Ability to Deal With Conceptual Issues Effectively

A large percentage of the work done in focus groups is exploratory, whether dealing with new products or new ideas that are being evaluated for advertising, promotion, or packaging. Often the groups will require the use of techniques that are oriented toward encouraging the participants to think conceptually about the topic being discussed and to visualize ideas that are not well developed. Some moderators are very capable of dealing with this type of session due to their own abilities to work effectively with abstract ideas rather than concrete issues. Others have difficulty conducting effective focus groups unless the material covered is concrete and the outputs expected from the participants are straightforward.

The Ability to Work Effectively With a Group Process

One of the major benefits of focus groups is the ability to use the energy of the participants to interact with each other so that the topic being discussed can be explored in greater detail than would be the case if the discussions were handled in a question-and-answer format. This requires the moderator to know how to involve the members of the group in the discussion in such a way that they will react to each other rather than simply responding to the moderator.

Some of the worst focus groups I have observed are structured more like question-and-answer sessions, with the moderator asking questions and the various people in the room providing responses to the topics. In essence, these types of focus groups are really individual interviews conducted in a group setting rather than focus groups because of the limited amount of interaction among the participants.

Ability to Change Course Quickly and Effectively

A well-trained, experienced moderator is able to realize when the group discussion is not working well (because of the nature of the questioning, the knowledge or attitudes of the participants, or the dynamics of the group) and is able to change the direction and put the group on a course that will accomplish the objectives of the assignment.

An example of this type of situation came in a series of groups I was retained to conduct for a bank seeking to understand its image among senior citizens in Brooklyn, New York. The goal of the research was to determine how the seniors felt about the special programs this bank had developed for the older people in an effort to attract them as customers. Within the first 10 minutes of the discussion, it was evident that the people in the group were completely unable to provide any point of view about the client institution. Although some of the people in the group had heard of this bank, they knew nothing about the organization.

We then proceeded to move to a discussion of special programs that financial institutions have to attract seniors to them, hoping to learn which programs these participants were aware of and what were the most important services from the perspective of the senior citizen. However, it quickly became evident that the people in this group were completely unaware of anything that a financial institution would provide for a senior that was not available to younger people in the market. At this point, a less experienced moderator would be in major trouble, as both key topics that were intended to be covered in the groups were identified but the participants had no knowledge of either. Therefore, the entire content of the discussion guide had been essentially covered, and the group had only lasted 20 minutes.

What to do? To provide assistance to our client, we chose to start at the beginning and talk with the seniors about what would be likely to attract them to a specific financial institution and how they had made decisions in the past regarding the financial services organizations with which they had done business. Then we discussed a variety of different types of special senior-oriented services that could be offered to these people, with the goal of determining which, if any, would have an impact on them in terms of their selection of a financial institution.

At the conclusion of the group, our client had obtained excellent information about the profile of its institution in the community (low) and the types of services that would appeal to seniors in the market, so they could begin developing marketing ideas for subsequent research that would ultimately be the basis for their special effort to attract the seniors in the area. What could have been a focus group disaster turned out to be a very helpful session.

The Ability to Remain Objective at All Costs

One of the most important characteristics of a successful focus group moderator is the ability to separate his or her own biases from what occurs in the group. The moderator must be able to listen to the output from the discussion in such a way that his or her interpretation of the information obtained from the participants is not affected by a need to please the client or by a bias that this individual has about the topic when going in. I have experienced many client situations in which we were presenting a selection of items to a group (new positioning ideas, new product concepts, new packaging graphics, etc.) and the client asked me, before the sessions began, which I felt was the best of the lot. Most clients are surprised when told that one of the most important things the moderator can do is *not* develop a preference at the start about anything being discussed in a group, as this will become obvious to the participants and the result will be a bias in the group results. A moderator can have a dramatic effect on the way an idea is received by the group simply by the way it is presented in terms of both verbal and nonverbal inputs. Therefore, maintaining complete objectivity throughout the process is vital to effective moderation.

Understanding How to Read Nonverbal Reactions of the Participants and How to Use Them to Facilitate Group Discussion

Often it is possible to use nonverbal responses from individuals within the group to help gain insight into how they really feel about the topic being discussed. For example, if an individual is exhibiting behavior that suggests boredom with the topic, the moderator might call this to the person's attention and try to understand what is missing for this individual that might make the information more interesting or important to him or her. Similarly, sometimes a participant is not volunteering his or her opinion about a topic but clearly shows nonverbal signs of either excitement or boredom. This would provide a sign to the moderator to call the person's attention to the attitude he or she is suggesting so that this individual's views can be shared with the group.

Understanding What to Do With the Information Generated From Focus Groups So That It Provides Maximum Benefit to the Client Organization

There is more to moderating focus groups than simply being able to run effective sessions and write a report that provides an accurate summary of the findings. The most effective moderators are able to add value to the research project by providing perspective on what the findings from the focus groups mean in the context of the client company's overall marketing objectives. In addition, these moderators can provide specific recommendations for action on the basis of the conclusions that have been developed. This is one capability that few moderators can provide to clients, for the facilitator must have experience in the line marketing functions covered by the groups if the recommendations are to be realistic and believable.

Consequently, many people feel that the best background for focus group moderation is line marketing management or strategic marketing consulting. People who have this type of background have generally been integrally involved in the development of marketing plans and the various implementation steps that are necessary to get a new product or service into the market and sustained as a viable business. Therefore, this type of person has the practical experience to apply the output from a focus group program to the real-world marketplace, which is ultimately what the client will need to do with the information that was generated from the research.

Moderators often are asked about the best background for a career in focus group facilitation by people who think that psychology, social work, or sociology might be the best course to follow. Although all of these fields should give an individual training in dealing with human interactions and perhaps even some experience working with group dynamics, they all lack the practical hands-on experience that one gets from working in marketing, advertising, or marketing consulting. The moderator in such human relations fields might be an effective facilitator but would not be able to provide the quality of in-depth recommendations that would be expected from someone with line experience in marketing.

An Understanding and Complete Appreciation for the Confidentiality That Is Integral to the Focus Group Process

Although the work of a moderator can be extremely interesting and most stimulating, and thus an interesting topic to discuss with friends, family, and other colleagues, it is vital that this not happen at any time. A moderator must respect the confidentiality of the information with which he or she is working and *never* share any information generated from a focus group with others. Further, the moderator must understand that the information obtained in a focus group or the client inputs needed to prepare for this group should be considered insider information and not shared with anyone else for the purpose of investing in the client organization.

In summary, it is apparent that certain personal and professional characteristics are common to the most successful focus group moderators. These people are hard working and flexible and are patient, attentive listeners. They have excellent communication skills and the ability to analyze and apply a great deal of diffuse information, always with an eye to the marketing and business implications of the research.

6

PREPARATION FOR MODERATING

This chapter will discuss the most important tasks that a moderator is required to perform before the actual focus group sessions in order to maximize the likelihood that the research will be successfully implemented. Each of the areas covered represents a vital part of the process, as it can make the difference between effective research and focus groups that were judged to be a waste of money.

In the first part of the chapter, we will address the moderator's task of preparing both him- or herself and the client for the sessions to be conducted. Much of this is contained in a focus group research proposal, which is generally the document that the moderator develops in order to be assigned the business. In addition, most research requires some advance client briefing of the moderator so that an effective discussion guide can be developed, and this chapter will discuss the nature and importance of this activity. The second portion of the chapter will discuss the selection of focus group facilities—both how one finds the facilities in a particular market and how to contract with a facility to assist in the execution of groups. The third section addresses participant recruiting, one of the most important factors in the success of a research effort. Specifically, this will cover how participants are recruited, what the role of the moderator is in this process, and what types of actions a moderator can take to increase the chances that the groups will be recruited according to specifications. Finally, this chapter will address some of the most common recruiting obstacles and issues and what a moderator can do to minimize the chances that they will become a problem.

THE PROPOSAL

The preparation for moderating a series of groups actually begins before the project has been approved. A large percentage of qualitative research projects are assigned to moderators on the basis of the presentation of a proposal, which may have been developed as a result of a face-to-face meeting with the client organization. Whether or not the moderator actually meets the client in advance of the proposal (via phone, via Internet, or in person), this document is key in the initial stages of preparing a client organization for the focus group process. A well-developed proposal contains at least the types of information discussed below.

A Statement of the Specific Objective(s) of the Research

As stated in an earlier chapter, this is a very important part of the overall research process, as it becomes the driver for how the research will be conducted and what types of information the client is seeking to achieve from the groups. Ultimately, it is against this stated objective that the research project will be judged to be a success or failure. By including this in a written proposal, the facilitator is able to obtain buy-in from the key people in the client organization regarding the objectives of the sessions so that there will not be questions at the completion of the project as to what types of information the facilitator was trying to obtain. Further, it provides a means for the client personnel to react and provide feedback in the event that the objective is not completely accurate so that it can be modified and incorporated into a revised proposal.

An Indication of the Scope of the Investigation

This section of the proposal is an important part of preparation, as it outlines the types of topics the moderator anticipates covering during the groups. If written correctly, it should serve as a very preliminary, rough outline of the content of the discussion guide that will eventually be developed. From the moderator's perspective, this section is important because it sends a message to the client organization early in the process as to the general types of information that are likely to be covered in the research and serves as the basis for the more detailed discussion guide.

A Discussion of the Key Implementation Details

This portion of the proposal gives the client organization the information needed to understand how the groups will be recruited, who will be in the various sessions, where sessions will be held, and what the process is for developing documents such as the recruitment screening questionnaire, the discussion guide, and the final report. Specifically, included in this section are at least the following types of information:

- *A description of the types of people that will be recruited for the groups.* This is vital in that the client organization must agree with these profile criteria before any work commences on the research effort. Therefore, the section will provide a description of the participants who will be recruited and how the actual composition of the various groups will differ, based on the going-in objectives of the study.
- *The planned timing of the groups, in terms of the dates and times of the sessions.* This is particularly important in that it enables the client organization to organize the schedule so that the appropriate people can attend. This is often one of the most difficult parts of the overall planning process in the group process, for it can be very problematic trying to coordinate the schedules of many different people.
- *A discussion of the number of sessions that will be included in the research and the markets where they will be conducted.* This prepares the client for the scope of the work to be implemented and also enables them to have a better understanding of the cost elements that are out-

lined later in the proposal. Occasionally, this section may also include information about the specific facilities where the groups will be held, although most client organizations are comfortable leaving this information up to the moderator, under the assumption that the moderator will know the best place to hold the sessions. After the client has approved the project and the moderator is involved in further implementation steps, it will be necessary to provide the client with directions to the facilities where the groups will be held, recommendations for local accommodations, and instructions on when they should arrive and how to ensure that they maintain their anonymity when coming to the facility.

- *Information regarding the discussion guide, in terms of when it will be developed and the process that the moderator will use to develop it.* It is often an excellent idea to include in this section a list of the types of information that will be requested from the client organization so that the appropriate people can begin planning to obtain the information or material needed to develop the discussion guide.

- *Availability of choices regarding the taping of the sessions,* which is important to the client in terms of planning their on-site involvement. For example, if the groups are to be audiotaped *and* videotaped, some people may choose not to attend the sessions but rather to watch the tapes at a later date. This also would be a "heads up" for the client if the client wanted to involve many different people in the research because videoconferencing might be the most cost-effective way to address this need. In addition, the use of videotaping usually increases the total cost of the project and may affect the client's decision on how to proceed. In any case, this section gives the client important information needed to make plans regarding the groups.

- *A discussion of the type of final report that will be developed as a result of this research and when the client organization can anticipate receiving this document.* This is important in that clients sometimes have very specific requirements as to the types of reports they need or the time when they need the document.

- *A project approval and implementation time line.* It is often important to incorporate into a proposal a detailed time line so that the client organization considering the research can determine if it can adhere to the type of plan that is being considered. For example, does the schedule of approvals necessary to meet the anticipated start date correspond with the capabilities of the organization, or will adjustments have to be made to accommodate the needs of various key people in the client organization? Alternately, will the planned schedule provide the client with the findings in adequate time to meet its internal needs?

- *A summary of the costs and billing information associated with the research.* This final section typically outlines the costs of the research and any other extra costs (travel, special taping, etc.) that will be expected as part of the program. In addition, this section should identify the anticipated payment schedule so that the client organization can do the planning necessary to get the moderator paid.

THE FACILITATOR BRIEFING

The purpose of the facilitator briefing is to provide the moderator with the background information necessary to develop an effective discussion guide, conduct a productive session, and ensure that the moderator is sufficiently familiar with all the objectives of the research so that key areas to be probed are not ignored when they are brought up in a group. The need for and scope of a facilitator briefing vary considerably depending on the extent of the relationship between the moderator and the client organization, the advanced knowledge that the moderator has about the topic being discussed, and the complexity of the topic area.

For the purpose of this discussion, we will assume that the moderator does not have a close working relationship with the client organization, that the topic to be discussed is relatively complex, and that the moderator does not have a good understanding of this area before the meeting. In this situation, the facilitator briefing would include the following elements:

- *An introduction to the key people in the client organization who will be involved in the research effort.* This is important because it enables the moderator to hear the goals and biases of the various people who will come to the groups, review the results, and implement the actions coming out of the groups.

- *A discussion of the overall objectives of the groups, with the goal of trying to reduce these objectives to the simplest possible statement to which everyone can agree.* This is the statement that should be used in the proposal when the moderator states the objectives of the research. The goal of this part of the briefing is to ensure that the objectives are as singleminded as possible and can be achieved using the methodology that has been proposed.
- *A review of the methodology for implementing the groups.* If only focus groups are to be used, this should be reviewed again to ensure that all interested parties are comfortable with this decision. Further, if more than one methodology will be used in the research, then it is important that everyone in attendance agree that this is the most appropriate way to accomplish the research objectives.
- *Detailed background on the topic area to be covered by the groups.* The client organization should provide sufficient background information so that the moderator can develop a reasonable understanding of the areas that will be covered in the groups. The intent of this briefing is *not* to make the moderator an expert but rather to give this person enough information to develop a thorough discussion guide and ask the right questions during the session as probes to responses that are generated from the participants.
- *A review of the time line that has been outlined in the proposal.* This needs to be included in the briefing to ensure that everyone involved in the process understands the requirements for the completion of the various deliverables in the process.

SELECTING THE FOCUS GROUP FACILITIES

Most contractual arrangements between clients and moderators normally require the facilitator to select the facility where the groups are to be conducted. Occasionally, a client organization will have a bias toward or against a facility and will ask or insist that the moderator follow specific direction relative to selection, but this is very rare. Most client organizations realize that moderators have facilities in the major markets with whom they have developed a relationship over time and that it is in the best interest of the research not to insist on a specific local research company.

The selection of the facility is a very important part of the overall research process, for a poor selection can result in the implementation of unsuccessful groups. The criteria that are generally used when selecting a facility include the following:

- *The ability of the facility to recruit qualified participants* is the most important characteristic relative to facility selection. This is relevant only if the facility is given responsibility for recruiting (which is often the situation), as there are other options that will be discussed later in this chapter. The moderator must be sure that the facility can deliver the requisite number of qualified participants at the appointed time for all groups to be conducted at that facility.

- *The location of the facility* also is often very important. This is because moderators and clients want the convenience of proximity to airports, railroad stations, major highways, or branch offices of the client organization. The right location can make the travel easier, making the total project more efficient, and can also facilitate the best quality recruiting.

- *The physical plant of the facility* is very important to some people in client organizations, who need to have excellent viewing facilities (i.e., large one-way mirrors) and very comfortable seating arrangements. Further, some facilities are more conducive to high-quality audio and video recording than others, and this can be very important to a client for certain types of research.

- *The professionalism of the facility staff* can also be an important issue when selecting a place to hold the groups. Some organizations use only part-time help (often high school or college students) to staff their facilities while groups are in session, and these people often are not sensitive to the needs of the client or the moderator before, during, or after the group. This lack of experience and sensitivity can hinder the flow and efficiency of the process, making the overall project a less-than-positive experience.

- *The costs charged by the facility* also can be influential to a moderator when selecting a place to hold groups. Although there generally are not major differences in costs among facilities, sometimes the assumptions (incidence of finding qualified people, co-op monies—that is, honoraria for participants—needed to motivate candidates to come to the groups, participation rates among people who qualify, etc.) made by the local research companies are very different, which can result in a wide range of fees quoted for a single project. Often these differences can be somewhat neutralized by ensuring that all facilities asked to bid on a project are working from exactly the same specifications and with similar assumptions.

- Finally, occasionally a facility will be selected partially on the basis of *the quality of food, beverages, and snacks it provides to the client observers*. This should not be an important criterion in the overall selection process, but to some people it is a very significant part of the overall focus group research process. The responsibility falls to the moderator to ensure that no unnecessary discomfort or disappointments will interfere with the client's satisfaction with the project.

LOCATING A FOCUS GROUP FACILITY

Almost every major city in the United States and around the world now has at least one focus group facility. In most cases, the difficult part of the selection process is not locating qualified facilities but rather finding the one that meets most of the criteria discussed above. Most moderators tend to use the same facility (or two) in a market on the basis of good prior experiences with this organization and the desire to build a relationship with one company so that it understands and can anticipate the needs of the moderator. This can save considerable time when planning the groups in terms of directing the facilities on requirements for rescreening, room arrangements, and so forth.

If a moderator is required to conduct groups in a market where he or she does not already have prior relationships, there are three principal ways to locate a facility:

1. Communicate with colleagues in the industry who may have conducted groups in the market. This is generally the best and most reliable way to find a facility, as it is based on firsthand knowledge of the organization.
2. Confer with client research people, who may identify a facility in a market where they have had a successful prior experience. Some

moderators are reluctant to ask their clients for facility recommendations, as it might appear that they are not in control of the process; however, this can be an effective way to find a good facility in a market in which the moderator does not frequently work.

3. Use some of the available secondary source materials that provide listings and/or ratings of focus group facilities throughout the United States. The most popular of these publications are

The Green Book, a publication of the New York chapter of the American Marketing Association. This publication can be obtained by calling the organization at (212) 687-3280. It provides a comprehensive listing of facilities by market, along with the facility's address, phone number, and major principles and a brief overview of its capabilities.

The Impulse Survey, a relatively new resource for finding focus group facilities, and one that is becoming more important each year. It contains much the same information as the *Green Book* but also includes a rating of the facility on seven characteristics and recommendations for nearby hotels. The facility ratings are based on inputs provided to the publication by moderators following their use of the facility. This publication can be obtained by calling the Impulse Research Corporation at (310) 559-6892.

Quirk's Marketing Research Source Book, an ancillary publication of *Quirk's Marketing Research Review,* a monthly magazine that focuses on the quantitative research industry. It provides a listing of the focus group facilities in each market but does not generally have the same breadth or depth of information about them as is found in both of the above publications. This directory can be obtained by calling the magazine at (614) 854-5101.

THE PARTICIPANT RECRUITMENT PROCESS

If the right people are not in the focus group room, you can have the best moderator and the most thoroughly developed discussion guide, but the results from the groups will be essentially worthless. One of the most important lessons learned when conducting qualitative or quantitative research is to ensure that the information is obtained from the right types of people, in terms of their qualifications for the group and representation of the population toward which the client organization wishes to direct its efforts.

In addition, when recruiting focus groups, it is essential that enough participants come to the sessions so that the process can have an opportunity to be maximally productive. If moderators across the United States (and perhaps the world) were asked to describe their biggest concerns when planning groups, most probably would refer to the recruiting process—both the qualifications of the participants and the show rate for the session. There are few more embarrassing moments for a moderator, when a group is about to begin, than having only two or three people (of the 12 recruited) waiting to start the session.

The purpose of this section is to discuss the recruiting process in order to provide moderators with the tools needed to maximize success in recruiting the groups.

The Recruitment Organization Options

There are essentially two approaches to recruiting most focus groups: using the focus group facility to implement the recruiting for the moderator and contracting with an independent recruitment organization to find the people. In very rare situations, a client organization might do the recruiting, but this is normally limited to employee groups, educational groups (i.e., recruiting students or faculty from one institution), and some customer groups.

Most moderators use the focus group facility to handle the recruiting, as it is one less organization with which to coordinate on the focus group process. In addition, this choice places responsibility for all aspects of the field implementation of the sessions in the hands of one organization, thus making a successful research experience more important than if two companies shared the assignment. The independent recruitment organizations tend to be used by moderators who believe that these organizations are needed to find very specific types of people (e.g., physicians, computer specialists) or to recruit in markets where they are not confident that the local facility can perform this function credibly.

The Elements of the Recruitment Process
and the Moderator Role in Each

Recruiting focus group participants involves four very distinct phases, which are integral to the process whether the recruiting is managed by an independent organization or by the local focus group facility. This section will discuss the phases and the role that a moderator must assume to make sure the process works effectively.

Establishing Recruitment Parameters

This first step in the recruitment process should always involve discussions between the moderator and the client organization to clearly define the types of persons that are needed for the various sessions. As indicated earlier in this chapter, the general recruiting specifications will be outlined in the proposal; however, it is essential that they be reviewed in detail once again when the recruiting process is ready to begin in order to ensure that they still represent the most current thinking of the client organization. A key part of this discussion is the identification of the co-op payment that will be used by the recruitment organization so that the client understands what assumptions have been built into the cost structure. If the moderator or the recruitment organization is not confident about the probable success of recruiting full groups with this co-op amount, the client should be notified at this stage that it may be necessary to increase the co-op payment.

*Development of the Recruitment
Screening Questionnaire*

This is a document developed by the moderator for use by the recruitment organization in finding people qualified for the groups. Although there are many variations in the content of recruitment screening questionnaires, the sections that are common to almost all are

- An *introduction* in which the recruitment organization seeks to find the right person to talk to by asking a few basic questions that relate to the most general specifications.

- A *security and participation* section in which the prospective candidate is asked about prior involvement in focus groups, as some clients will not accept people who have participated in some previous number of months. Further, the participant is asked a question or two that relate to security, as the goal is to protect the confidentiality of the material in the groups by not having people in the room who could benefit (or help others to benefit) from the information discussed.

- A *series of attitude or behavioral questions,* aimed at finding people for the groups who meet the appropriate specifications on the basis of their knowledge of a particular topic or their use or purchase of a good or service.

- A *demographic summary,* in which the participant is asked basic age, income, and family size questions, as these often are important criteria that must be met for the person to qualify for the groups.

- *An articulation question,* which is used for some types of groups. This is a general question asked to ensure that the participant is sufficiently articulate to be a viable member of the group. This also will help screen out people with language problems or speech defects. An example of an articulation question often used is "Please describe where you would build your next home and why you selected this location." It is the type of question that requires some thinking but is not threatening to anyone with a reasonable command of the English language.

- *The invitation,* a request for the qualified person to attend the groups, with an indication of how much he or she will be paid and the time and date of the sessions. If the person agrees, he or she is given the actual location and directions as needed.

A sample recruitment screening questionnaire for a consumer group involving rice is shown in Table 6.1.

MANAGEMENT OF THE FIELD RECRUITMENT PROCESS

It is possible to have the best moderator, the most effective discussion guide, and the most well-thought-out stimuli and have completely un-

Table 6.1   Sample Screener Survey

Name:_____ Home Phone:_____

Home Address:_____

City:_____ State:_____ Zip:_____

Hello, I'm _____ from Focus Plus, an independent
market research firm in Manhattan. We're conducting a survey among people in the
area, and I would like to ask you a few questions.

Q1. Sex (by aural observation)
       Female   **continue for Groups 1 & 2**
       Male   **continue for Group 3**

Q2. Which of the following groups includes your age?
       Under 25   *terminate*
       25-29   *terminate*
       30-39   **continue**
       40-49   **continue**
       50-54   **continue**
       55 or older   *terminate*

Q3. Are you the primary grocery shopper, or do you share the shopping duties for
       your household?
       Primary   **continue**
       Shared
       Not involved   *terminate*

Q4. Do you or does anyone in your household work for any of the following
       industries—advertising, public relations, or marketing research—or for a food
       manufacturer, distributor, or retailer?
       Yes   *terminate*
       No   **continue**

Q5. In the past 6 months, have you participated in a group discussion or survey for
       market research purposes?
       Yes   *terminate*
       No   **continue**

Q6. Which of the following food items have you purchased in the past month?
       (READ LIST)
       Cereal
       Crackers
       Bread
       Boxed Rice   **MUST RESPOND POSITIVELY OR TERMINATE**
       Canned Vegetables
       Fresh Produce
       Deli Meat

(continued)

Table 6.1   Continued

Q7. Which, if any, of the following products have you purchased in the past month? **(READ LIST)**
   Any Whole-Bean Coffee
   Terra Chips
   Any Extra Virgin Olive Oil
   Knorr Soups or Mixes
   Newman's Own Spaghetti Sauce or Salad Dressing
   Any Fresh Pasta
   Boboli–Fresh Pizza Kits
   Any Bottled Water
   Any Flavored Tea
   Wolfgang Puck Frozen Pizza
   Paul Prudhomme's Magic Seasoning Blends
   Bread Du Jour
   Wick Fowler or Carroll Shelby Chili Mix
   Contadina Refrigerated Pasta Sauce
   Fantastic Foods or Nile Spice Soup in Cups
   Lindt, Tobler, Droste, Ghirardelli, or Godiva Chocolate
   Marie Callender Frozen Dinners
   Trio's Pasta Sauces

   MUST RESPOND POSITIVELY TO 3+ OR TERMINATE

Q8. Which of the following best describes the number of times during an average week that you prepare a meal for your household? **(READ LIST)**
   None   *terminate*
   1-2
   3-4
   5-6   **continue**
   7 or more

Q9. Which of the following best describes the number of times during an average month that you either go out to eat at a restaurant or get carry-out food to bring home to eat? **(READ LIST)**
   None   *terminate*
   1-2
   3-4
   5-6   **continue**
   7 or more

Q10. Which of the following best describes the average cost of an entree at the restaurants and/or carry-out establishments you patronize?
   Under $15   *terminate*
   $15-$20
   $20-$25   **continue**
   $25-$30
   Over $30

Table 6.1   Continued

Q11. During an average month, please tell me the number of times you personally consume each of the following foods? **(READ LIST AND RECORD #)**
   Some type of potato
   Some type of rice
   Some type of pasta
   Some type of poultry
   Some type of red meat

The following questions are for classification purposes only.

Q12. Which of the following best describes the number of family members living in your household? **(READ LIST)**

1	*terminate*
2-4	
5-7	**continue**
8 or more	

Q13. Which of the following best describes your total household annual income? **(READ LIST)**

Under $30,000	
$30,000-$49,999	*terminate*
$50,000-$74,999	
$75,000-$89,999	**continue**
$90,000 or above	

INVITATION
We would like you to come to our facility in Manhattan for a group discussion regarding food products. This discussion will be held at Focus Plus on November 2 at 2:45 p.m./5:45 p.m. (WOMEN)/7:45 p.m. (MEN) and will last approximately 2 hours. We are not trying to sell you anything. We only are interested in your opinions. For your participation, we will give you a cash incentive of $60 (5:45—and dinner will be provided). Would you be willing to participate? (If yes, record information on first page of screener. If no, thank and terminate.)

---

successful focus groups. This can occur if there are not the right number of fully qualified people at the facility when the groups are to start. Even though the recruitment implementation is handled by organizations that are subcontracted by the moderator, from the perspective of the client organization, the responsibility for recruiting lies in the hands of the moderator. Therefore, it is essential that moderators take a very active role in the recruitment process to ensure that problems do not threaten the integrity of the groups and that they be available to the subcontractor organization to solve problems that arise when the recruiting is not proceeding according to plan. This section will discuss the types of actions a moderator can take to minimize the likelihood of avoiding recruitment problems.

Before the Recruiting Begins

Before the actual recruiting starts, there are a few key steps the moderator can take that will normally help ensure a smooth process of finding qualified candidates:

- Provide sufficient time for the recruitment organization to find the people for the groups. Many of the problems that occur in recruiting are created by moderators (and/or clients) who do not realize that it can be difficult to find certain types of people and that timing is important to an effective process. Even though most facilities have many people doing the recruiting, it is not reasonable to expect that they can dramatically staff up for one rush job to meet a specific quota, as this could hamper their ability to fill groups for several other clients.

- Develop a recruitment screener that is easy to understand and simple to implement and that includes only the most essential information needed to find the correct people for the groups. Some client organizations like to use the recruitment screener as a mini-quantitative survey and therefore put in extra questions about topics that are of interest to them. These ancillary questions simply add costs and timing to the recruitment process and probably are of little real value to anyone due to the small sample size on which the data are based.

- Ensure that the recruiting organization understands the screening parameters and is completely comfortable with the wording and flow of the questionnaire.

- Be sure that the recruiting organization tells the candidates to come to the facility at least 15 minutes before the groups are expected to begin. This is very important, as most people tend to be late, and the 15-minute cushion should help account for this so that sufficient people are in attendance when the sessions are scheduled to begin.

While the Recruiting Process Is Proceeding

When the recruiting actually begins, the moderator should become very involved in the process, with the objective of ensuring that no unsolved problems emerge that will threaten the viability of the groups. The specific actions the moderator should take during this process are:

- Maintain regular contact with the recruitment organization(s) by requiring them to provide a daily spreadsheet that indicates the basic characteristics of the people who have been recruited to date. Essentially, the moderator should identify the three or four most important criteria and make them banners on the spreadsheet so that it is easy to get a quick overview of the people who have been recruited and how they fit with the screening characteristics.
- Review the spreadsheets daily to ensure that the people who are recruited meet the specifications and that any questionable recruits are investigated to ensure that they are acceptable.
- Provide the spreadsheets to the client organization (project contact individual) every few days to secure their agreement on the quality of the people who have been recruited. This will enable the moderator to identify problems from the client perspective in time to correct them so that the project does not become compromised.
- The moderator must also be responsive to problems in the recruiting that may require some modifications in plans. For example, sometimes it is necessary to open up the recruitment criteria—that is, to loosen the parameters—if a specific restriction is inhibiting the process to the extent that it could threaten the ability to fill the groups. For example, if the client wants to find men between 30 and 45 who use a product to reduce the gray in their hair and it becomes apparent that this product would be used more by men over 45, it may be necessary to broaden the age target to 50 or 55 to find the appropriate candidates for the session.

Another common problem relates to purchase criteria for a particular product. For example, perhaps the client is seeking to talk with women who have purchased skin moisturizers more than four times in the past year. During the recruitment process, it is reported that most of the apparently qualified candidates terminate on this question, as women tend to buy larger sizes and therefore purchase this product only two or three times per year. Therefore, it may be necessary to reduce the requirement in order to fill the groups with acceptable, qualified participants.

A final issue that frequently emerges from the recruitment process and requires a decision is the amount of money budgeted for the co-op. This is the one area of the focus group process in which the moderator/client and the facility can be working toward somewhat different objectives. For example:

- It is in the best interest of the facility to use the highest co-op remuneration possible, as it will make the recruiting easier and therefore lower the facility's internal costs of recruiting the groups.
- On the other hand, the client and the moderator are interested in keeping the co-op at the lowest possible level, as it is an expensive part of the focus group process and one that they would like to control.

In light of the above, when issues associated with raising co-ops occur, they often become a source of concern and annoyance to the client. Some clients are not familiar with the costs associated with recruitment, so when they are asked to raise the co-op from $X to $Y, they feel this is because the recruitment organization is not doing their job effectively. However, we have found that sometimes it is very difficult to determine the right amount of money to use as an honorarium before the actual recruiting begins, keeping in mind the interests of both parties. Normally, we will take the policy of starting with a lower amount but recognizing that it may be necessary to increase it if people are unwilling to participate for this fee.

At the End of the Recruitment Process

The most important action that the moderator can take during the last 24 to 48 hours before the groups occur is to ensure that the facility has filled all the requisite quotas and that it has an effective process in place to confirm and reconfirm that the candidates intend to come to the group. Last-minute cancellations and no-shows can be disastrous to a focus group, and the moderator must take whatever action is possible to prevent this from happening. The obvious action is to over-recruit the group by two to four people, under the assumption that some people will not show up and others may cancel at the last moment. Unfortunately, this can become costly because if more people show up for the group than are used, they have to be paid and sent home.

The moderator should be sure to talk with the facility on the day of the group to ensure that everyone has been contacted again to confirm his or her participation and that the recruiters have identified more people than are needed to cover the no-shows and last-minute cancellations.

At the Facility, Just Before the Groups Begin

During the 15 to 20 minutes before the groups are scheduled to begin, the moderator should be in regular contact with the receptionist at the facility to see how many people have arrived. Because the screener indicated that the people should come 15 minutes before the session is scheduled to begin, the moderator should have an excellent assessment of the status of the recruiting by 5 to 10 minutes before the session. This will determine whether the group can start on time (i.e., if enough people are in attendance) or whether it is necessary to wait for others to arrive. In the event of a shortfall, the moderator will be faced with an important decision as to when the group must begin for the required topics to be covered in the time allotted.

If there is a problem with last-minute cancellations or no-shows for the first group, the moderator might ask the people at the focus group facility to call the candidates for the second group to remind them about the session. This could avert a real problem if the recruiters who originally contacted the candidates did not impress on people the importance of their attending this session.

SUMMARY

The buck really stops with the moderator in the focus group recruitment process. If problems occur, the moderator will be held accountable for them. Therefore, it is essential that a moderator anticipate problems that may occur in the recruiting process and take corrective (or preventive) actions that will minimize the risk that these problems will threaten the viability of the groups.

7

RECRUITING PARTICIPANTS

One of the biggest mistakes that can be made in the focus group process is to choose the wrong people to participate in the focus group sessions. Although this may seem obvious, and although some readers may feel that this situation could never happen, it occurs much more often than many professionals in the field probably would like to admit. The objective of this chapter is to discuss the focus group recruiting process and to explore many of the decisions that need to be made during the planning phase of the research to ensure that the participants in the room are optimal in light of the goals of the research. The chapter will first focus on the types of actions and decisions that a moderator can make to increase the probability that the participants in the room will be the right people and then explore some of the biggest problems that moderators have with the recruiting process and what can be done to minimize or even eliminate the chances of their occurring.

AN OVERVIEW OF PARTICIPANT RECRUITMENT

Before discussion of the role of the moderator in the recruitment process and the types of decisions that need to be made to ensure that everything happens according to specifications, it is necessary to briefly describe the recruitment process in terms of the steps in the process and how the recruiters find the participants for focus groups.

The first step in the recruitment process (once the markets for the sessions have been determined) is to determine the specifications of the people who will be in the groups. These must be committed to writing so that there are no questions about the demographics and so that other relevant characteristics are known before the process commences.

The second step in the process is the development of the recruitment screening questionnaire, the document used by the recruiters to find the most appropriate people for the groups. A detailed discussion of the recruitment "screener," as it is called in the industry, was provided in the previous chapter.

The next step in the process is the communication of the information in the screener to the organization that will be doing the actual recruiting. Normally, this is done via phone, mail, or e-mail; however, in situations where the recruiting is particularly complicated, it may be necessary to brief the recruiters in person.

The actual recruitment of participants is the next step in the process, and the one that generates the most questions and comments from people who are peripherally involved in the focus group process. Specifically, the issue raised is generally how the recruiters find the participants for the focus groups. Essentially, participants are located in three primary ways:

1. Using *lists* that the client organization might provide the recruitment organization or that the client might direct recruiters to procure. It is very common for clients to have lists of customers or prospects that they want to be used as the source of the recruitment to make use of the specific characteristics of these people and the objectives of the research.

2. Using *data banks* of names that a recruitment organization has developed. A data bank is a collection of names that have been developed and catalogued in a computer for future use in focus group recruitment. It is not unusual for an organization to have a data bank of 25,000 or more names that include consumer, business-to-business, and medical candidates. The common characteristic of everyone in the database is that the people have been contacted before and have agreed to participate in focus groups if they qualify. Therefore, when the recruitment organization gets an assignment, the first step is to try to recruit participants from the data bank, as this is the most efficient and effective recruitment method. It is also a very effective tool, for the recruitment organization knows how often the person has been asked to be involved in a group, so it can control the frequency with which the individual is used as a participant.

3. *Random recruitment.* In a situation in which the specifications for a particular group are relatively unusual and the recruitment organization does not have sufficient people in its database, it is necessary to go into the market to find the people. For example, if a client is interested in talking with owners of flower shops that are members of FTD, it will be necessary to use local phone books to call these retail outlets and try to recruit qualified participants. Random recruitment is not as cost-effective as data bank recruiting because participation rates among qualified candidates will be lower among individuals who have not previously agreed to come to a focus group. Therefore, it is necessary to recruit more people in this scenario to account for an anticipated low show rate.

4. *Low-incidence recruitment.* Occasionally, a client organization is interested in conducting focus groups in a target market segment that is very difficult to find because of its low incidence in the population and the absence of obvious ways to locate qualified participants. An example might be men who chew tobacco, women who drive trucks, or teenagers who take a particular drug for acne treatment. In these types of situations, it is not unusual for a recruitment organization to advertise in local newspapers or community bulletin boards to find participants, with the goal of motivating the people to call in to determine if they qualify. This is a very expensive way to find focus group participants, but it is sometimes the only viable way to find qualified people.

The next step in the recruitment process is the follow-up with the candidates who agree to come to the groups. In most cases, a recruitment organization will provide both fax and telephone confirmations before the group as a reminder to the individual about his or her participation.

The final step in the process is the rescreening of participants when they arrive at the focus group facility. Essentially, this is a process of asking the people a few key questions to ensure that they qualify on the basis of the specifications of the groups. This process will be discussed in more detail later in the chapter.

THE MODERATOR'S ROLE IN THE RECRUITING PROCESS

In most situations, the moderator must act as the project manager in the recruitment process in terms of ensuring that the various steps in the process have been executed properly so that the right people come to the groups. Most clients expect the moderator to handle the recruitment of participants and will hold this person accountable for poor recruiting, even if the less-than-satisfactory recruiting was caused by the subcontracted recruitment organization. As a result, it is essential that the moderator understand his or her role in this process and be able to manage this process to avoid problems. The following will summarize the key actions that the moderator must take to maximize the chances that the recruitment effort will be successful.

Determine the Recruitment Specifications
With the Client Organization

This is one of the most important functions a good moderator can perform for his or her clients, as often organizations do not think through the characteristics of the participants as thoroughly as they should. Importantly, even when the moderator is provided with specifications by the client organization, it is essential that he or she review them to ensure that they are correct. For example:

- Often clients wish to talk to the decision maker in an organization about a topic being discussed in business-to-business groups. Although this might be the right person, in many situations, the better person to include in the sessions is the *significant influencer*—the individual in the organization who does the research and analysis regarding a purchase decision and then presents the results to the executive who makes the ultimate decision. If the client organization is interested in understanding the dynamics of the purchase decision process and the factors that are influential when considering various options, the ultimate decision maker probably will not be very helpful because he or she did not get involved in this aspect of the process.

- A client may be seeking inputs from men about a particular type of clothing, such as underwear, socks, or a scarf. Although men are the obvious target for this type of product, research shows that a large percentage of these products are purchased by women for men, so the specifications might be better if they included both men and women as potential participants in the groups.

- A client may want focus groups on a brand or type of beer, which is generally consumed by men. Though it is important to talk to men about their views regarding the product or category, it is well known that a large percentage of beer is purchased by women for men. Therefore, the client might well get a much more thorough understanding of the overall decision process for purchasing this type of beer if women were included in the research.

Determine the Most Appropriate
Composition of the Groups

Because of the importance of group dynamics to the focus group process, it is vital that the composition of a group be considered very seriously, for the wrong approach can significantly inhibit the participation or create problems in the group that could have been avoided. For example:

- Depending on the topic being discussed and the general nature of the participants, the age differential among the participants can be important. In most situations, it is advisable not to cross generational lines within a group, so a person who is 25 should not be in a group with someone 50. This is too wide an age spread and normally will not be conducive to good group discussion.

- Sometimes, it is advisable to separate males and females in a group. With teenager sessions, it is essential to do this, and even with some adult topics the group dynamics will often work much better if men and women are not involved in the same session.
- It also is generally advantageous to have people in the same group who have relatively similar experiences with the product or service in question or similar demographic or purchase characteristics that would lead them to be relatively similar with regard to the topic being discussed. For example, if groups are conducted to learn about attitudes toward specific weather-forecasting sites on the Internet, it is important to talk to people who do and do not access these types of sites in separate sessions. This is because the depth of the information that will be obtained from the discussion in the sessions among people who do access the sites will be greater as a result of their common experiences. Further, among the people who do not access these sites, the moderator will be able to probe much deeper into why they do not go to them (assuming that participants are aware that the sites exist) and what might be done to motivate them to try some of these sites. In addition to the importance of homogeneity to the efficacy of the group discussion, it also is much easier to analyze the results of the groups if the same types of people are in each session because one can focus on the result of the entire group discussion rather than having to concentrate on the specific outputs of different participants due to their unique attitudes or behavior.

Develop an Effective Recruitment Screening Questionnaire

The screening questionnaire is particularly important because it is the primary way that a moderator can communicate with the people who handle the recruiting to ensure that they understand what types of people are to be recruited for the groups. Also, this questionnaire can have a significant impact on the cost of recruiting for a focus group, as it will determine the number of people who qualify among those who are contacted. The recruitment screener was discussed in detail in the previous chapter.

Manage the Recruitment Process From Beginning to End

One of the biggest mistakes that a moderator can make is to assume that once the screener is provided to the recruitment organization, everything will go according to plan. The recruitment of participants is probably the most problematic part of the entire focus group research process because of frequent inappropriate recruiting (i.e., selecting people who do not meet the specifications) and high no-show rates on the day of the groups. As a result, it is important for the moderator to be in regular touch (daily if possible) with the recruitment organization so that the process can be managed.

Develop an Effective Rescreening
Process on the Day of the Groups

Despite the best efforts of a recruitment organization, it is always an excellent decision to develop a brief rescreening questionnaire that can be administered to the participants when they arrive at the facility. This should ensure that the people who have been recruited are who they said they were to the recruiter and that they really meet the specifications.

MAXIMIZING THE PROBABILITY OF EFFECTIVE RECRUITING

This section will identify the most important points a moderator should keep in mind to achieve successful recruiting. Although there is no way to guarantee perfect recruiting for a group, by following the guidelines in this section, the chances for filling the groups with the right people will be dramatically increased.

- Develop realistic screening criteria so that it will be possible to find the types of people who are required with a reasonable effort. Some organizations tend to get so specific with the recruitment guidelines that it becomes almost impossible or extremely costly to find the types of people to include in the sessions.

- Use a recruitment organization in which you have confidence, and do not select it only on the basis of price. There is generally not a meaningful difference in the prices charged by different organizations to recruit groups, so the key criterion should be the insurance one gets from knowing that the right people will be found for the sessions. Any incremental costs of using a more expensive organization will be more than offset by the problems one will face if the groups are poorly recruited.

- Recognize the need to recruit more people than you will actually use in a group, realizing that if everyone shows at the facility, you will have to pay people whom you do not include in the group. The number of people to recruit for a group will vary dramatically depending on the demographics of the participants. For example, if you are recruiting teenagers, it is generally necessary to invite almost two people for each person that you will use. On the other hand, if you are recruiting nonworking housewives, you can often recruit 11 or 12 and be very confident that 10 will show for the session.

- Ensure that the key people in the client organization have seen (and concurred with) both the recruitment specifications and the screening questionnaire. They must agree on the types of people that will be included in the groups, or it will be difficult to convince them to accept the findings from the sessions, particularly if these findings are not consistent with their going-in objectives.

- Maintain regular contact with the recruitment organization so that problems in the process can be addressed as early as possible to avoid a crisis on the day or two before the groups. It is not uncommon for a moderator to check in with the recruiting organization on the day before a group, only to find that sufficient people have not been found to fill the groups. At the last minute, often little can be done to resolve this situation, so it is vital that the moderator stay in touch with the organization throughout in order to anticipate problems that appear to be evolving.

- Be prepared to relax some screening criteria or to pay more for the co-op if the recruitment organization is having difficulty filling the groups. Although this is not the optimal scenario, it is often necessary in order to identify sufficient people to discuss the subject in the groups.

- Be sure to rescreen all participants when they come to the facility. This process should be done by the facility personnel in an area that is away from the main sign-in desk, as each individual must be rescreened separately to avoid the possibility that one candidate will copy the responses from another.

THE MOST COMMON RECRUITMENT PROBLEMS AND HOW TO REDUCE THEM

It is very difficult to organize focus groups without having some problems with recruitment, as this is the one area in which neither the moderator nor the recruitment organization has complete control over the process. There is no way to guarantee that a participant who was recruited for a group will actually show up at the facility at the appointed time. However, if one has a good understanding of the problems that do occur, it is often possible to take actions to minimize them before or during the recruitment phase of the project. The following are the most important problems we have faced in recent years and what can be done to minimize them.

Not Enough People Show up at the Groups

Low show rates are a moderator's nightmare, as they are very visible to the client and can result in less-than-satisfactory sessions. To minimize the chances of having unsuccessful show rates, the moderator can do the following:

- Significantly over-recruit the groups, recognizing that it may be necessary to pay some people who show up but do not participate in the sessions.
- Maintain *daily* contact with the recruitment organization for the 2 weeks prior to the groups to monitor the progress and to make adjustments as needed.
- Increase the co-op payments to higher than normal levels (normal varies considerably depending on the nature of the people being recruited) in order to increase the incentive of the people who have been successfully recruited to come to the groups.

Too Many of the Participants Have Been in Focus Groups Before, With Possible Effects on the Representativeness of the Information Generated

Frequent participation by respondents is one of the biggest issues in many client organizations, as they feel very strongly about using "virgin" or near-virgin respondents. If it is important not to have people with a history of focus group participation in the groups, the moderator can do the following to reduce the incidence of these types of people:

- Invest additional money in the recruitment process to recruit only for new participants. This can be extremely expensive and may even be impossible to accomplish in some product categories (i.e., professional, medical, business-to-business) because of the size of the universe from which the facility can recruit.
- Include in the recruitment screener a past-participation notification, with the caveat that the answer must be true or the person will not be paid if he or she come to the facility. Specifically, prospective participants must know that their past participation will be checked by the facility and by a third-party organization that exists for this purpose and that if errors are identified in the answer, the participant will be dropped from consideration for future groups. To achieve this, however, requires the cooperation of the focus group facility.
- Include questions within the first 10 to 15 minutes of the actual group discussion that will seek to determine whether the person has participated in the past. A participant generally will not expect the moderator to ask these types of questions and will feel that because the group has begun, there is nothing that can be done to him or her. However, if the moderator finds violators on the basis of the participant's responses in the preliminary discussions, this person can be removed from the group and sent home without payment.

Participants Come to the Groups Late, So It Is Not Possible to Start on Time, or the Moderator Must Admit People to the Room Late

This also is a very common problem, but one that often can be easily corrected. The most common way to fix the problem is to tell the participant that the group begins 15 minutes before the actual start time so that latecomers will actually arrive in time for the start of the session. In the case of participants who understand the focus group process and come late intentionally in order to be "paid and sent," the moderator can do one of two things:

- Refuse to pay anyone who comes more than 15 minutes late.
- Require the "late" participant to sit in the waiting room until the group is over before receiving payment.

Although neither of these will affect the group being conducted, if more moderators would take this posture, the participants would be more diligent about arriving on time.

Participants End up in the Groups Who Do Not Meet the Specifications That Were Outlined in the Screener

This also is a relatively simple problem to correct, as it simply involves the implementation of a comprehensive rescreening process when the participant comes to the facility. Essentially, the candidate is asked several key questions (from the original screener) to ensure that he or she meets the criteria. Although it is possible for people to lie or stretch the truth in order to qualify, the moderator can handle this situation in the same way as the past-participation issue discussed earlier, by asking key questions during the early part of the group to determine the extent to which the participants are telling the truth about their screening answers.

Participants Who End up in the Group Are Either Too Shy or Not Articulate Enough to Be Effective

This is one problem that should occur very infrequently if the moderator has taken the appropriate precautions during the recruiting and the rescreening process. Specifically:

- A screening questionnaire should contain an articulation question (described in an earlier chapter as a simple question that requires the participant to talk about a subject for a few seconds so that the recruiter can determine if he or she is sufficiently articulate to be in the group) so that obviously nonqualified candidates can be eliminated from consideration.

- It is also very helpful to provide guidelines to the facility personnel who do the rescreening so that they know what to look for when interviewing the candidates. Some moderators leave very precise directions on not accepting anybody who has a speech problem or an accent or who appears to be very shy when signing in and therefore can eliminate these people before they come to the groups.

In summary, focus groups' success or failure to a large extent depends on the quality of the recruiting process. Starting with a clear definition of the criteria and following through to the design of the screener, the source of names, and the thoroughness of the recruiters, a good moderator will shepherd the entire process to ensure that the participants are the right ones for the project.

In terms of demographics, psychographics, product usage, and the ability to articulate responses, each participant must be considered an essential building block of any successful focus group project.

8

PRE- AND POSTGROUP BRIEFINGS

In an earlier chapter, we discussed the importance of the moderator's preparation for focus groups, and we outlined many different actions that an experienced moderator will normally take to be ready for the groups. One aspect of this pregroup preparation is the briefing of the people who will be observing the sessions to ensure that they get the most out of the groups. The purpose of this chapter is to discuss three stages of the client briefing process, each of which is a very important part of the overall process of making the research effort successful for both the moderator and the client observers.

CLIENT PREPARATIONS BEFORE THE DAY OF THE GROUPS

Once the strategic aspects of a focus group project have been completed, two important elements of the client preparation phase must still be addressed before the day of the groups. One is giving the client organization implementation instructions to help ensure smooth execution of the groups. The other is clarifying the goals of the research to the client observers to increase the probability that they will be in a state of mind that is conducive to good listening and learning when they come to the groups.

Implementation Instructions

In the interest of the smooth execution of the research, it is very important that the moderator advise the client about the following execution details that relate to the activities that will happen at the focus group facility.

Everyone who will be observing the focus groups from behind the one-way mirror should arrive at the research facility at least 45 minutes before the groups are to begin. This is important for two key reasons:

1. It avoids the possible interaction of an observer and a focus group participant in the event that they both arrive at the focus group facility at the same time to check in with the receptionist. Most focus groups are more effective if the client sponsor can remain anonymous for at least the beginning of the sessions, and this anonymity can be destroyed before the group begins if a client observer comes to the reception desk and announces that he or she is from XYZ company and is there to observe the groups.

2. It enables the moderator to conduct an effective pregroup briefing with all participants. The format for this will be discussed in detail later in this chapter.

To help ensure confidentiality, the client observers should remove all forms of corporate identification before they arrive at the focus group facility. Many companies require employees to wear identification badges to gain access to their offices, and it is not unusual for observers to forget to take off their badge before they get to the facility, a lapse that could alert participants to the nature of the research and client. Also, some people enjoy wearing or carrying logo merchandise from their employer, and this also can signal to the participants who is sponsoring the research. Clients should also ask for the moderator or the moderator's company when coming to the facility so that they do not reveal the name of their organization if participants are in the same area when they check in.

Moderators should also make sure that the client contact person has advised all client participants of the following specific details:

1. The location of the facility, including directions
2. The hotel where the client contact and perhaps the moderator are staying, to facilitate coordinating transportation in out-of-town markets
3. The time the groups will start and the time that the observers are expected to be at the facility
4. The number of groups that will occur
5. The plans for serving meals to client observers, if appropriate
6. The importance of asking for the moderator or the moderator's company when coming to the facility, so they do not reveal the name of their organization in the event participants are in the same area when they check in

Although these may seem to be obvious instructions that would normally be provided to the appropriate people in a client organization, it is my experience that often observers come to a facility without removing corporate identification, or they arrive late to a group because they have stopped for something to eat, not having been told that food would be provided for them at the facility.

Clarifying Goals of Research

The second major aspect of client preparation before the day of the groups concerns clarifying the goals of the research. It is very important for the moderator to ensure that everyone who will be attending the sessions has a basic understanding of the objectives of the research and of the types of information that will be obtained as a result of the sessions. It also is often an excellent idea to involve the prospective observers in the focus group preparation process by seeking their inputs early in the process as to what information would be useful to get from the groups and what segments of the population would be best to talk with in order to get it. If this type of preparation is not taken within the client organization, the moderator can be faced with serious problems during the briefing session for the group. Although some moderators take the position that they can be accountable only to the specific contact person within the client organization, more experienced moderators will anticipate problems and provide the guidance to their immediate contact so that potential problems with others in the organization can be avoided.

PREPARATION ON THE DAY OF THE FOCUS GROUPS: SETTING UP THE BACK ROOM FOR THE CLIENT OBSERVERS

It is a useful practice for the moderator to arrive at the focus group facility well before the client observers to ensure that the appropriate details are arranged in advance to facilitate the assimilation of the client people into the process. For example, the moderator should

- Alert the facility receptionist that approximately "X" people from the client organization will be coming early and that they should be escorted to the back room when they arrive.
- Ensure that the actual focus group room is set up properly so that the group can proceed without problems when the participants arrive. This means that pads and pencils should be on the table, appropriate easels and chair rails should be ready for showing materials, and, when the groups are to involve exposure to audio or video material, the equipment should be in place and tested. In addition, refreshments for the participants should be available in the discussion room.
- Arrange the back room so that it is most conducive to effective viewing, with paper and writing implements available for all observers and with sufficient quantities of the discussion guide and participant spreadsheets available for the participants to review before the start of the groups. Some moderators also like to make the recruitment screeners available in the back room if there is a question about whether a participant is appropriate for the group.

THE PREGROUP BRIEFING

The first purpose of the pregroup briefing is to ensure that the client and moderator are united as to the purpose of the research and the methods to be used to gather information. The second purpose is to provide the observers with the tools necessary to help them get the most out of their involvement in the groups. The following are the primary subjects that the moderator should address in a pregroup briefing:

- *The research objective*—It is very important that the moderator begin a briefing with a restatement of the objectives of the groups so that the observers understand the goals that the research is intended to achieve. Occasionally, client observers will come to focus groups with their own hidden agendas about what is to be obtained from the discussion, and the specific statement of objectives can be very helpful in avoiding conflicts stemming from different going-in perspectives.

- *The role of these groups in the overall process*—The people who will be observing these groups should understand the dimensions of the research process and how these groups fit into the project. This includes a summary of the total research plan, which may include a quantitative phase or other kinds of exploration, and how the findings are to be used. In some cases—if, for example, the groups are the fifth and sixth in the series—the pregroup briefing should explain what has occurred thus far in terms of the number of groups, the specifications of the participants, and the most important findings that have emerged thus far. Further, if additional groups are to be included in a series, the moderator should identify when and where they will be conducted and what the nature of the participants will be.

- *The recruitment process and the characteristics of the people who will be in these groups*—Client observers often find the recruitment process to be somewhat mysterious, as they wonder how the "moderator" goes about finding the people who come to the groups and, even more important, why people are willing to participate in a focus group. Therefore, the pregroup briefing should include a short discussion of
  1. The characteristics of the people who will be in each of the two groups to be held that evening and why these specifications were selected
  2. The process that is used to recruit, in terms of whether the people come from lists provided by the client to the moderator or from data banks at the facility or other resources for finding qualified candidates

3. The remuneration that is paid to the participants as an honorarium for coming to the groups
4. The anticipated number of people who will be included in each group

- *The most important administrative details associated with the focus groups,* including
  1. When food will be served
  2. The location of the bathroom facilities
  3. The existence of the one-way mirror and the importance of keeping the lights out in the back room
  4. The need to keep the noise level very low in the back room, as the sound can be very distracting to both the moderator and the people in the group
  5. The recognition that the participants will be told that there are people observing the sessions in the back room, although the specific identities of the observers will not be revealed

- *The way communications will occur between the moderator and the back room observers during the session*—This can be a very touchy area, particularly in situations in which the client and the moderator have not worked together before. As indicated in an earlier chapter, I believe it is very important that the interactions between client and moderator during a focus group session occur in the back room and not in front of the participants. To this end, a periodic trip to the back room by the moderator during the course of the groups is the best way to keep the discussion on track. Because this is not what all clients expect, it is wise for the moderator to explain the reasons for this approach before all groups and to emphasize that notes sent into the room are not acceptable, except in a emergency (whatever that would be!). This is vital to the success of focus groups, as the moderator must be in control of the entire process. As part of this discussion, it is also helpful for the moderator to explain that there is a limited time available when he or she comes to the back room and that those people who wish to share thoughts should do so clearly and concisely so that the moderator can assimilate the question or information into the discussion with little problem.

- *Tips for the observers that will enable them to get the most out of watching the groups.* Some key areas that are helpful to share with the observers are

1. The importance of looking at focus groups from a macro rather than a micro perspective, in terms of focusing on the big issues that come from the discussion rather than the small points. This is not to suggest that it is not possible to get an important insight from the comment of one person in a focus group, but rather to encourage observers to try and concentrate on getting the sense of the group in relation to the most important issues for which the research is being implemented.

2. The value of focusing on listening rather than writing during the group. Some people watch a focus group and try and write down every detail they heard that was important. As a result, they often lose sight of the overall sense of the group because they were so intent on writing that they really could not do any quality listening.

3. The importance of keeping the discussion among the observers in the back room to a minimum, as the more the people talk among themselves, the less they can listen to the comments of the participants.

4. The importance of keeping an open mind when listening to a focus group. It is very common for people to come into a focus group with a point of view about the topic being discussed and to use the output of the group primarily to confirm their belief. Although there is no way to stop this behavior, by acknowledging the possibility that it could exist among some of the observers, the moderator will make people aware of this bias and hopefully motivate them to try and listen to the session more objectively than they might otherwise.

- *The discussion guide.* The moderator should conduct a three-part review of the discussion guide with the client:

1. The moderator should explain the purpose of the guide (providing a copy to each of the observers) and how it will be used during the group. Essentially, the moderator wants to communicate that he or she will cover all the material in the guide but will also deviate from the outline if the group discussion leads in a direction that the moderator thinks may be important to the objectives of the groups. At the same time, the observers should be reassured that if the moderator moves away from the content of the guide, he or she will always return to the guide structure when the diversion has been completed.

2. The moderator should review the flow and content of the guide, walking the client observers through the various sections of the guide and explaining briefly their purpose and how the material will be handled. The purpose of this portion of the pregroup briefing is to ensure that all the observers are comfortable with what will be covered during the group discussion. A key objective of this briefing is to obtain a buy-in from the observers that the right material is being covered in these groups in light of the goals of the research. As part of this discussion, it is helpful to identify the opportunities during the group when the moderator might come to the back room to talk with the observers. In this way, if someone in the back room has a pressing issue to communicate, he or she will know when to expect the opportunity to talk to the moderator.

3. The pregroup review of the moderator guide should include an explanation of the "external stimuli" that will be used during the group, including the role of the material in achieving the goals of the groups. It is also important for the moderator to explain to the observers how the groups are to be exposed to the stimuli and why this is the best way to do this in light of the nature of the stimuli and the objectives of the research.

- *Revisions or additions to the original guide.* The pregroup briefing is also an optimal time to identify whether some of the material in the guide should be presented differently or whether any areas should be eliminated or added. As indicated earlier in this book, one of the greatest benefits of the focus group process is the dynamic nature of the methodology, which enables the moderator to make significant changes in both content and approach from one group to another. As a result of this, people who observe the first groups in a series should be alert to the possible need to make changes in the guide to increase the effectiveness of subsequent groups in a series.

- *Questions from the client.* The moderator should leave adequate time for the client observers to ask questions about the focus group process, the participants, the discussion guide, or the external stimuli before the groups begin. This enables the observers to get any questions or issues they have about the research addressed before the sessions begin so that they can focus on the output from the participants rather than being distracted by other related topics.

THE POSTGROUP BRIEFING

Most clients like their moderator to provide a very short debriefing after the day's focus groups in order to share with the observers some preliminary thoughts about what has been learned so far and the plans for the future. The postgroup briefing can be a very helpful part of the overall process, but it can also become very destructive if not handled properly. For example:

- This can be a useful 15 to 20 minutes if the moderator is able to clearly articulate key impressions from the information generated to date. As a result of this brief overview, the moderator can determine the extent to which there is agreement on findings that have emerged up to that point. Also, this short briefing will often help the moderator identify the areas that need to be covered in more detail in subsequent groups to ensure that the client observers understand the issues that will ultimately be raised in the focus group report.
- The postgroup debriefing can be particularly important after the first two groups in a series, as this is often when changes in content or approach are discussed as a way to improve the overall quality of the material generated by the research.
- On the other hand, if a moderator is not careful in his or her approach to the content of the postgroup briefing, the observers may feel that the moderator already has a point of view about the outcome of the research and therefore cannot be objective about subsequent sessions. Therefore, it is important that a moderator preface all comments in the postgroup discussion by saying that these are preliminary thoughts based on an immediate reaction from the group and that his or her opinions might change significantly after the rest of the groups in the session are completed.

There are a few important *do's and don'ts* for the moderator's performance in the postgroup discussion. The moderator should

- Summarize the key findings from the groups as accurately and factually as possible.

- Maintain a posture of complete objectivity relative to the ultimate conclusions and recommendations.
- Ensure that the client contact person and the observers at the groups are comfortable with both the content of the guide and the approach used to elicit the information from the participants.
- Be willing to make appropriate modifications in the research approach if it appears that there are other ways of achieving the objective that will not compromise the integrity of the moderator or the research process.

The moderator should *not*

- Draw any conclusions or make any recommendations during the postgroup discussion, even if the moderator has begun to formulate what the report ultimately will say. The reason for this is that it may appear to the clients that this conclusion is premature, based on partial findings, and therefore of questionable value. Also, by providing this type of information, the moderator loses the leeway to modify the thinking after reflection, review of the notes, or relistening to parts of the tapes.
- Use this time to propose more research, as this would be inappropriate. Although the outcome from the day's groups might suggest a need for additional research, this recommendation should be presented as part of the final report rather than as a "pitch" after the groups. Experience indicates that such a proposal carries more weight when presented as part of the recommendations in the report than when presented following the groups.

KEEPING TRACK OF INFORMATION
DURING A FOCUS GROUP SERIES

One of the biggest challenges facing moderators arises when a series of groups are conducted over several days in different locations. At the end of such a series, it can be very difficult for a moderator to organize notes, materials, and observations and to do an effective postgroup briefing. Therefore, I generally record the most important information obtained during a focus group on my copy of the discussion guide and write a detailed memo for the file within 12 hours of the completion of each segment of groups, using my notes (and my memory) as a guide. The intent of this file memo is to put down on paper all the relevant information that the moderator has collected from the prior day's groups so that I can use this as a reference in the future when talking to clients about the research or when writing the report. I find that the most effective format for these notes is to follow the discussion guide outline, writing down the key points that emerged relevant to each area. At the end of the document, it is also helpful to include a section that identifies the key unanswered questions to date and what the moderator anticipates doing to obtain the answers as the research effort proceeds.

Some people who use this approach will even share this information with their key client contact, as it is helpful to identify areas of agreement and disagreement and to determine the specific subjects that will need to be covered more effectively to meet the requirements of the research.

In summary, a successful focus group moderator understands how to manage the process for maximum productivity. This does not imply any manipulation of the information, but rather the execution of details to ensure that the client personnel who attend the focus groups are appropriately briefed to get the most out of the process. An experienced moderator will never assume that the observers at the groups have been fully briefed about the effort being undertaken or that they agree with the approach. Instead, a successful moderator will manage the pregroup preparation and then the briefing process to anticipate and thus avoid potential problems. Ongoing communication with the client organization before, during, and after the groups helps focus group research to most effectively achieve its objectives.

9

THE DISCUSSION GUIDE

This chapter will discuss the principal research instrument used by focus group moderators to direct the flow of the session. Specifically, we will cover the purpose of the discussion guide and the process that should be used to develop it; then we will review the various sections of a prototype guide that can be used to exemplify a typical format.

THE ROLE OF THE DISCUSSION GUIDE

The discussion guide has two primary roles in the focus group research process and some secondary purposes. The actual role that a discussion guide plays in the research process depends on the relative level of importance that the moderator and the client organization ascribe to it. In this context, views differ as to the importance of the discussion guide in the overall process, with some moderators feeling that they do not want to be encumbered by a document as formal as the typical discussion guide and others recognizing that the guide is a very useful part of the focus group process that can help to ensure that the output from the groups is consistent with the anticipations of the client. Because I feel strongly about the importance of developing a thorough and comprehensive guide, the focus of this chapter will be in this direction. This is because an experienced moderator will not be constrained by the content of a guide, as he or she will have the confidence to deviate from the material when appropriate but at the same time will have the benefit of a detailed outline that can be used to focus the thrust of the discussion, in keeping with the client objectives for the research.

Both of the two basic roles that a discussion guide fulfills in the focus group research process are extremely important to the achievement of success with the research effort. The first role is as a vehicle to facilitate communications between the moderator and the client organization. By developing a comprehensive discussion guide, the interested parties at the client organization will have an opportunity to see what types of material the moderator anticipates covering in the groups, so they have the opportunity to offer suggestions for change. Without this means of communication, it is almost impossible to ensure that both the moderator and the client personnel will have complete agreement as to the nature of the discussion that will occur during the groups. Another major benefit of the discussion guide for the client organization is that this document enables multiple persons within the company to feel a part of the research process, as they can be exposed to the guide in advance of the groups and have the opportunity to offer their thoughts about the most appropriate content or the emphasis that is anticipated for each segment. With this type of involvement, it is generally much easier to gain acceptance for the final output from the research because the various people have an ownership investment in the content of the groups.

The importance of the moderator guide as a communications vehicle with the client organization cannot be overestimated, so it is essential that the moderator treat the development of this document as a serious part of the process. For some people in the client organization, it is the first exposure they get to the focus group process that will be undertaken, and it can serve to form their opinion of both the moderator and focus groups in general. In addition, the discussion guide is one way that a moderator can demonstrate to his or her client the ability to think carefully and thoroughly about the particular topic being investigated, thus showing some of the added value that a bright, well-trained moderator can bring to the process.

The second key purpose of the discussion guide is to direct the flow of the conversation during the actual group. If this document is developed correctly, the moderator will know what topics to cover during the group and approximately how much time should be allocated to each. This is particularly important for relatively new or inexperienced moderators, as controlling the timing of a group is often a significant problem for them. In these circumstances, too much time is spent on the early topics, and the moderator is forced to rush through the later parts of the guide, which often is the most important material to be covered. Although some moderators feel they do not need a "crutch" such as a discussion guide, and others feel inhibited with this type of structure, experienced professionals will understand how to draw on the benefits of having an outline for the groups without feeling that they cannot deviate from the content in order to delve further into a topic that emerged from the discussion but was not anticipated during the planning phase of the research.

The discussion guide also has two other roles that are important to the overall focus group process. One is to provide a vehicle to indicate closure on the topics that should be discussed during the groups. Specifically, when the content of the discussion guide has been covered, the focus group should be over, and the various people observing the session should be in agreement. Without the document as a guideline, the moderator might have difficulty gaining the agreement of the people in attendance that the material that was anticipated to be discussed during the groups has been covered in accordance with the agreement before the groups.

A final role of the discussion guide is that it can be a very effective outline to be used by the moderator when writing the final report. Because the guide represents the topics that everyone agreed should be covered, if the text of the final report follows the same outline, then it should be an acceptable way to present the findings from the groups. In effect, the guide predetermines the structure of the final report that will be used to present the output to the client organization.

DEVELOPMENT OF THE DISCUSSION GUIDE

The process of developing the discussion guide will depend heavily on the nature of the relationship between the moderator and the client and the general familiarity of the moderator with the topic being covered in the research. For example, if the moderator is implementing focus groups on a topic with which he or she is extremely familiar and it also is a topic that has been done before for the client organization, the discussion guide development can be a simple and quick process that involves updating previous material to meet the requirement of the current research. However, if a moderator is not particularly familiar with the topic and/or does not have a long-lasting relationship with the client organization, the development process normally will include the following steps.

First, the moderator and the client organization hold an initial meeting (or telephone discussion) to agree on the objectives in the research or simply to confirm those that were identified in the proposal. There follows a briefing for the moderator, in which the client organization provides the following types of information:

- A more detailed discussion of the objectives of the research, from the perspective of why it is needed, what they hope to get out of the participants' inputs, and how the information from this research will be used.

- The key factual information that the moderator will need to know in order to have sufficient knowledge to develop the discussion guide, to have a complete understanding of the subjects that will be raised in the groups, and to probe specific areas during the discussion. Although it is beneficial for the moderator to have had some prior experience in the subject area, an experienced moderator will generally have the ability to grasp the essence of a new product or service area sufficiently well to perform effectively as the facilitator of the session. In fact, if the group felt that the moderator was an expert, they might well question his or her unbiased stance in the process (e.g., whether he or she was really an employee of the sponsor) or they might feel a need to use technical jargon when discussing the topic so they would not look stupid in front of this expert. Therefore, it is important that the moderator not appear to be an expert in the field being discussed but rather seem a reasonably knowledgeable individual who can ask the right questions and is seeking to learn from the participants.

A draft discussion guide is then developed by the moderator, based on the inputs provided in the briefing. This guide should be as complete as possible, with the assumption that it will be sufficient for the facilitation of the groups without any further input from the client organization.

Next, the draft discussion guide should be provided to the client organization for review and comment. This is an important part of the overall focus group research process, as it is the time when the client has the greatest opportunity to provide guidance and direction to the moderator on the specific aspects of the groups to be implemented. The goal of this phase of the guide development is to bring up all the important issues concerning the upcoming focus groups so that the moderator can benefit from the inputs of the client organization regarding both the subject matter of the groups and the time allocated to each of the topics.

Following the client inputs, the moderator should prepare a "final" guide and return it to the client to ensure full agreement with the approach that is to be taken. At this stage, it is assumed that the development of the guide is finished. However, an experienced moderator will continue to look for ways to modify the guide, along with the approach to the research, as the groups progress, as the learning from the early sessions can often be used very effectively to improve the overall quality of inputs from the later groups.

THE CONTENT OF A DISCUSSION GUIDE

There probably are as many different formats for presenting a discussion guide as there are moderators in the focus group industry, so it would be presumptuous to suggest that there is only one "right" format. Most moderators feel that the format they use is the best approach because it works for them and provides the type of guidance that will permit them to conduct an effective focus group session. Therefore, most moderators will work only from their own format, even if a guide has been developed by someone else. If they use someone else's guide, they will generally modify the format to meet their own style.

The discussion of the moderator guide that follows represents a format I have found to be very useful for more than 20 years. Although the content of the guide changes based on the subject matter to be discussed, the general format and approach to data collection has remained essentially the same for many years. The balance of this chapter will discuss the moderator guide in terms of the sections that are included, the flow of the discussion, and the use of timing within the context of the material.

THE SECTIONS OF THE MODERATOR GUIDE

The Introduction

This is a very brief section that is intended to set the stage for the groups in terms of the role of the moderator, the purpose of the sessions, and the ground rules for the sessions. This section should contain the following specific elements:

- A statement by the moderator introducing him- or herself to the group and using this opportunity to emphasize the role as facilitator and not category expert. This is the time in the group when the moderator begins to develop rapport with the group, so it is important to be friendly but firm and authoritative in self-presentation.
- A brief discussion of the general purpose of the group so that the people in the room understand what they will be doing and what is expected. For example, the moderator could indicate that the purpose of the group was to understand how the participants used the Internet for research and then to expose them to a new product that might be helpful to them in this effort. This type of introduction sets the participants up for the expectation that they will be asked about their current Internet search behavior so that they can begin thinking about this area. It also alerts them to the fact that they will be seeing a new product later in the group, which should help keep their interest level high for quite some time in anticipation of this exposure.
- Administrative details of the groups and the "rules" that apply. This is when the moderator might indicate the existence of the

mikes to tape-record the sessions, the one-way mirror, and the videotaping (or videoconferencing) of the groups. It also is appropriate to indicate to the participants in this part of the guide that there are people watching the groups from behind the one-way mirror. Most moderators will not say exactly who is observing the sessions (as it could affect the confidentiality of the work) but rather they indicate that there are colleagues back there taking notes and observing the proceedings. Many moderators find it helpful to make light of the one-way mirror so that it does not appear to the participants that they are being spied on by observers. If the mirror is handled effectively by the moderator, it will be completely ignored by the participants and not be a factor of any kind in the overall group discussion.

- Introduction of the participants to the group. The type of information provided at this juncture will depend heavily on the nature of the sessions and whether the group is a consumer, medical, or business-to-business research effort. Generally, the moderator will ask the participants to state their name and
  - For *business-to-business groups*, their company, title, and possibly a brief discussion of job function.
  - For *consumer groups*, their family composition and possibly some information about a specific product or service use.
  - For *kids groups*, their age, grade in school, and favorite product or activity that might relate to the topic being discussed.
  - For *medical groups*, their specialty or subspecialty, hospital affiliation, number of years in practice and perhaps a brief description of their patient population.

Data Collection

The second section of the discussion guide is the data collection part, where the participants are asked to complete one or two brief write-down exercises before the actual discussion begins. The type of information that would be collected at this juncture in the group would normally be very basic usage, attitude, or recall information that relates to the general product or service category that will be discussed during the groups. Some examples of the type of information that might be collected in a data collection section could be

- Information about the awareness of and attitudes toward a particular group of products or services that will be discussed later in the group
- Reactions from the group to the importance of specific characteristics when making a product purchase decision—also to be discussed later in the group
- Summary of the individual's purchase history for a particular product

Most moderators do not use this type of vehicle to bridge the gap between the general introduction and the initial group discussion, but it is a very useful tool for several different reasons. Specifically, it is a helpful way to focus the attention of the participants on the general area that will be discussed in the early part of the group, and it forms a transition between the participants' lives outside the focus group session and their activities in the group room. Further, such a section is a useful tool to collect some basic information from the participants that the moderator might use later to write the report or to serve as a reminder to the participants when the discussion covers the area later in the group. And by having this information in writing in front of the participant, there is less likelihood that participants will respond to a question with an answer geared toward what they feel the moderator wants to hear, or what would be popular in the group, rather than a reflection of their own views.

Even though this part of the group process takes only about 10 minutes (or less), clients or inquiring moderators often ask why the participants could not fill out this information in the waiting room while they were waiting for the group to begin. They are concerned that doing it in the group room wastes time that could be better used for additional discussion. However, there are a few important reasons why it is essential *not* to have participants filling out the forms in the waiting room, and to allocate the time during the group for this exercise. They are as follows:

- The moderator has no control over the interactions among the participants while they are filling out the forms. Ideally, these should be done independently so that each person's own views are considered. However, if the information is provided to people when they sign in for the group, it is not possible to be sure that each person has provided an answer that reflects his or her view rather than that of the person sitting next to him or her in the room.

- It also is essential that the participants in the waiting room do not talk about the topic area that will be discussed in the session before coming into the group room where they can be "supervised" by the moderator. This is because the seemingly innocent comments of one or two individuals in an unsupervised discussion could serve to bias some of the participants on the topic being discussed.

- There is often a need to explain how to complete certain parts of a form, and this should be done by the moderator who understand the purpose of the document.

- Finally, from a security perspective, it is important that all materials that relate to the group content be completed in the group room. Most focus group facilities use a common waiting room for participants, so one has no control over who is able to see the content of the specific form being completed by an individual. In view of the extreme importance of maintaining high levels of confidentiality in the groups, completing information forms in the waiting room would not be prudent.

Warm-Up Discussion

As a general rule, it is important that the flow of the discussion in focus groups proceed from the general to the specific throughout the session, with the material becoming more precise and directed to the topic area as the group progresses. The warm-up discussion section provides an important way to begin the group discussion, as it normally focuses on covering most of the material that was addressed by the participants in the data collection phase of the group. This should be the easiest and most general discussion of the area that will be explored in depth throughout the group. Because much of the information to be discussed was written down by the participants, they are normally very comfortable talking about it during this first section. The warm-up also is an "ice-breaker" for participants who might be reluctant to contribute to the group because the topics being discussed are very general and the moderator is working hard at this phase of the process to encourage full participation of all those in the room and interaction between individuals with different views or experiences about the topic to be discussed.

Subsequent Discussion Sections

After the general warm-up discussion, the moderator guide normally will include an additional three to five sections that are broken out on the basis of the subject matter to be covered. There are no specific guidelines for these sections other than the importance of adhering to the basic premise of moving from the general to the specific. As a general rule of thumb, the moderator should plan to allocate at least half the time in the group to the in-depth discussion of the specific topic to be covered. The warm-up and introductory sections are very important basic information that will lead up to the specific discussions about the particular topic for which the groups have been developed. It is essential that the moderator leave sufficient time to adequately cover the key topic, as there is often a tendency to try to include so much ancillary material in the early part of the groups that the discussion can become very rushed when the most important topics are to be covered.

The Final Section: Advice to the . . .

In almost every discussion guide I develop, the final section is titled "Advice to the . . . ," where the person advised could be the president, the director, the project manager, or anyone else that might represent a source of authority at the client level to the people in the focus group. The purpose of this section is to obtain from the participants a summary thought/reaction about the topic that has been discussed over the past 2 hours that communicates their own perspective on the topic in a way that might be helpful to the ultimate client. Over the years, this final section of the group, which is generally very short, has proven to be one of the most important parts, as it can provide the client with a sense of whether the information presented to the group was well received or requires significant additional work.

The most common way to introduce this part of the group is for the moderator to say to the participants that the group is almost over but that there is one final input that would be helpful to complete the process. The moderator then tells the participants to assume a scenario whereby the president, product manager, director, or other authority comes into the focus group room and asks for 30 seconds of their advice about the topic that was discussed that this executive could use to plan the direction of this effort over the next few days. For example, in the case of a new product, I would tell the group to write down what they would advise the project manger to do about this new idea as the future of this venture is considered. The key point to be made to the group is that they should share their personal views as to whether they feel it is a good or bad idea and what types of suggestions they want to make to the client organization. I find it helpful to give the participants the license to tell the client organization to save their money and give it to charity if they feel the idea is not viable. I also encourage the participants to provide suggestions to the client that might make the idea viable if these could be incorporated into the product or service area. This approach will work for virtually any type of focus group in which the participants are asked to provide their views about a new or existing product, service, advertising, promotion, or positioning idea.

Integral to this part of the group is the requirement that the participants write down their advice to the executive rather than simply be prepared to talk about it when asked. The write-down requirement is important as it will enable the moderator to elicit the real feelings of the participants rather than what they feel will be the popular view in the room. The way this is normally handled is to ask each person to read aloud what he or she has written as advice to the client person. Once this is completed, the moderator has one final opportunity to question participants about their advice in light of the views they have expressed during the group.

Historically, we have found that the summary comments from participants are extremely helpful in developing an overall sense of the feeling of the group relative to the topic being discussed. They also are a good way to end the session and provide a natural vehicle for the moderator to use with the client for a brief postgroup discussion.

BRIEF COMMENTARY ABOUT THE
WRITTEN FORMAT OF THE GUIDE

Over the years, I have found that the most effective discussion guides are written in a traditional outline form. The key to a successful format is that the topic areas to be discussed are separated into distinct sections of the guide and broken out into as much detail as possible in order to facilitate the communication between the moderator and the client organization and to serve as a reminder to the moderator regarding the areas that need to be explored. Though some moderators do feel encumbered by a very detailed discussion guide, the experienced facilitator will use the information only as guidance to help direct the discussion and to ensure that all the important topics are covered.

It is also very helpful in the guide outline to indicate when the moderator plans to use write-down exercises (discussed in detail later in Chapter 13) as part of the group process and when the moderator plans to formally use an easel to record inputs from the participant as a vehicle to stimulate discussion. By including this type of information in the body of the guide, the client observers behind the one-way mirror are given advance notice as to what will be happening in the group room and when they can expect to be able to communicate with the moderator directly. (Chapter 8 discusses the approach for moderator-client communication during the group.) This is helpful to the client observers, as they can formulate their thoughts and prioritize what they want to communicate with the moderator when this opportunity occurs during the session.

TIMING AND THE DISCUSSION GUIDE

An important element that is often not included in a discussion guide is the moderator's estimate of the time that should be allocated to each topic in the guide. This is a vital part of the discussion guide document so that the moderator can both ensure that all topics are covered during the session and communicate with the client organization during the guide development process about the amount of emphasis that is expected to be placed on the various topics to be covered. Without having an estimate of the time that will be allocated to each section of the guide, it is very difficult for the client to understand the depth of the discussion that will be conducted on a particular topic area. In addition, when people involved in the guide development process want to add material to the guide, they will have an understanding of the impact of the new material on the overall timing of the discussion and may have to agree to eliminate some parts of the discussion in order to be able to cover all the material in the groups.

TIMING GUIDELINES

As a general rule, a 2-hour focus group should be timed to go no longer than 1 hour, 45 minutes, because it is very common for sessions to start a few minutes late. Further, for the first session of the day, it is necessary to have some time to clean up the room between sessions. The planned timing of the guide should be indicated in parentheses at the beginning of each major section (e.g., 15 minutes) so that the reader will have no questions on the relative emphasis anticipated for each discussion area.

This chapter has covered the role of the discussion guide in the overall focus group process, how this key document should be developed, and what are the most important parts of a discussion guide that will facilitate successful groups. The most important message of this section is that the discussion guide should be viewed as a vital part of the overall research process, in much the same way as a client and its research organization would view a questionnaire as part of a quantitative research effort. Many clients are not as demanding of their moderators as they should be regarding the completeness of the guide and then find a need to become heavily involved in directing the flow of the discussion during the group because the key topic areas for which the focus groups were conceived are not being covered.

If the appropriate time and attention are placed against the process of developing a thorough discussion guide, and if the comments and approval process are utilized in the client organization, the observers of the group should be able to focus on absorbing the inputs from the participants based on the agreed-upon content of the discussion, rather than trying to redirect the efforts of the moderator to ensure that the most important topics are covered.

At the end of this chapter, we have included an example of a discussion guide written to explore attitudes of consumers toward a hypothetical new Web site. The format of this guide should be useful to the reader in developing discussion guides on other topics.

In summary, a comprehensive discussion guide that has been approved by the client is essential to productive focus group projects. The guide becomes the basis for agreement between the moderator and client on what issues are to be covered and serves to direct the moderator as the discussion flows during the groups. The guide itself should provide clear guidance on the flow, from introduction through data collection, discussion, and wrap-up, and should indicate the timing of each portion. With prior client approval on a detailed guide, there is little room for surprises or disagreements during the groups themselves, and the project can thus be maximally productive.

Discussion Guide for Company XYZ

Evaluation of a New Type of Cellular Communications Unit
(Conducted among current cell phone users who also have a personal electronic organizer)

I. Introduction (5 minutes)

Moderator

Purpose: To discuss cell phone usage, and to get your reactions to a new type of cell phone

Mikes, mirrors, and tapes

Confidentiality of the discussion

Introductions:

First name

Occupation

Type of cell phone owned

Type of personal organizer owned

II. Data Collection (10 minutes)

Ownership of and attitudes toward selected communications devices

Characteristics of the optimal cell phone

III. Warm-Up Discussion (20 minutes)

Discussion of current communications devices

Ownership of the selected items

Satisfaction with each

Discussion of how each of the communications devices can be made more effective

Importance of characteristics of the optimal cell phone

Discuss the reactions from the write-down

Identify which are the most important elements

— Determine why they are important

— Assess the relative value of each both in the absolute and compared to what they have with their current phone

Determine which characteristics are not important

— Understand why

— Identify if there is something that could make them more important

Probe need for such characteristics as Internet access, e-mail

Value of them

How they would be helpful

Determine if there are some characteristics that are important that were not included on the list provided

Identify them

Discuss why they are important

Determine the relative feelings regarding them and the most important elements that were included on the current list

IV. Introduction of the New Communications Device Concept Statement (40 minutes)

Pass out the concept statement for participants to read and evaluate

Overall reactions

In the absolute

Key strengths of the product . . . probing for:

— Value of the multiple devices in one

— Which are the most important elements, and why

— What features they do not want

— Reactions to the pricing

— Feelings about the size of the unit

— Importance of the power source

— Value of the guarantee

What is the most exciting part of this product?

Provide a description of the type of person that would purchase this item

Most important limitations of the device

What would preclude them from buying?

How could this be overcome

Issues with the price of the unit

Who do they feel would be the optimal manufacturer for this product?

Develop an unaided list with the group

Determine the reactions to each of the companies

    — Understand why they feel different types of companies are
       viable
    — Why would a telco be better or worse than a computer
       company?
    — Feelings about the product being manufactured by an organ-
       izer company (i.e., Palm Pilot, Casio, etc.) versus a computer
       manufacturer (i.e., Compaq, IBM, etc.)

V. Communications of This Device (20 minutes)

    Write-down exercise: Develop the headline idea for an advetise-
      ment that would effectively communicate the essence of this
      product

    Discuss the various inputs in order to identify the most important
      copy points that the participants made about the product

    Seek to prioritize the items to identify what will differentiate this
      product from all other communications devices

VI. Advice to the President (5 minutes)

New Cell Phone Concept Statement

Introducing a new concept in wireless communications technology that will revolutionize the way you operate in the new millennium. This new TotalCom cell phone is the complete communications solution for people who require full-service wireless communication, two-way paging, e-mail access, and a personal electronic organizer all in one small, lightweight portable unit. No longer do you have to carry several different electronic devices to manage your communications and personal organization needs. The TotalCom does it all . . . in just one unit.

This new product is only 8 inches tall, 5 inches wide, and 1 inch deep, and weighs just 6 ounces. Further, it operates on three AAA batteries, which should last 4 weeks or more depending on usage. The unit costs under $400 and carries a full-service 1-year warranty.

This product is available for sale at leading consumer electronics stores and can be ordered over the Internet from leading computer and electronics sites.

So move into the new millennium with the TotalCom. You will be glad you did.

Overall Reaction (10-Point Scale):

Strengths   Limitations

Ownership of and Attitudes Toward
Selected Communications Devices

Item	Ownership (Yes or No)	Satisfaction (10-Point Scale)	Comments (How could the device be more effective for you?)
Cell Phone			
Pager			
Electronic Organizer			
Device For E-mail Access			

Importance of Characteristics — Cell Phone

Characteristic	Importance (10-Point Scale)	Comments
Aesthetics		
Ease of Use		
Battery Life		
Reception		
Color		
Weight		
Price		
Ease of Recharging		
The Manufacturer		
The Warranty		
Existence of Special Features (address book, calculator, voice mail, paging, etc.)		
The "Feel" of the Unit in Your Hand		

10

EXTERNAL STIMULI

How many times have you heard that a picture is worth a thousand words? Well, in the focus group research business, this definitely is the case, as the picture (or another visual object) is often the catalyst for the group discussion that follows. The term *external stimuli* refers to objects that are introduced into the focus group research process to elicit comments from participants about specific topics of interest. Though it is not essential that a focus group session contain external stimuli, most do contain at least one type of stimulus. This is because researchers have found that participants can be much more helpful in a discussion if they are asked to respond to a tangible stimulus instead of trying to provide inputs to a verbal description of a product, concept, or idea.

TYPES OF EXTERNAL STIMULI

There are an infinite number of types of external stimuli, for by definition almost anything to which the participants in a focus group are exposed would classify as one. However, the following will describe the types of external stimuli that are most commonly used in focus group research.

Written Product Descriptions/Concept Statements

Probably the most frequently used type of external stimuli is a written description of a product, service, or conceptual idea to which the moderator seeks responses from the participants in the group. The objective of these statements is to describe the subject that participants will evaluate, in a neutral, matter-of-fact way rather than in selling language like that of an advertisement or sales brochure.

This type of stimulus, as it is traditionally used in a focus group, is given to participants, who are asked to read it and then comment (in writing or orally, depending on moderator preference) on the appeal of this particular idea to them.

Product or Packaging Samples

Another common type of external stimulus is an actual sample of a product or a package about which the moderator is seeking comments from the participants—for example, a new type of soft drink or a new approach to packaging for an existing packaged goods product such as a paper towel, can of soup, or box of pasta. By reacting to the item to be discussed, participants can provide their views regarding a variety of different elements, including perceptions of quality, value, taste, price, and target audience.

Frequently, the samples used have been made especially for the focus groups, using either computer technology to show a product or a package design or a model shop to produce a nonworking sample of the product. In either situation, the existence of the "real" sample is an effective way to generate useful inputs from participants that clients can use to evaluate their efforts to date and plan future activities.

Advertising Executions

One of the most commonly used types of external stimuli is advertising, which can be used in a focus group in a wide variety of different forms. For example:

- In some situations, the client wishes to do some exploratory research about some very rough ideas and might mock up a series of ads with a picture, a headline idea, and maybe one additional line of copy.
- Sometimes clients will want to have storyboards tested, with the soundtrack being provided by the moderator, their own person (which I do not recommend as an option), or even a tape that is played while the board is shown. I do not recommend having an outsider present the copy, as it brings another variable into the group situation that could have an impact on the ultimate findings.
- Frequently, the external stimuli will be an animatic version of a television commercial: that is, a filmed storyboard with a sound track, aimed at adding more realism to the presentation than occurs with a storyboard.
- In other situations, the people in the group are shown examples of print advertising, actual television campaigns, radio advertising, or billboards and are asked to provide their reactions.

Promotional Concepts

A common use of focus groups is to test the consumer interest in different types of promotions. Generally, they are presented to a focus group in the form of a concept board that normally will have a visual to depict the theme of the promotion, a headline idea to communicate the essence of the promotion, and copy to explain the promotion.

Internet Inputs

One of the most commonly researched areas in the current marketing environment is that of Internet-related products and services. For example, it is common to conduct research with consumers about a Web site and to access the site live in the group so that people can experience the content and full breadth of information available. This is a new category of external stimuli used in focus groups that will grow in importance in the future.

Participant Written Exercises

Chapter 13 extensively discusses various techniques used during focus groups to help the moderator delve deeper into the reasons why the consumers feel or act the way they do. Many of these techniques require the use of written forms or other types of write-down exercises, and all are a form of external stimuli, as they are an outside vehicle used to stimulate thinking and discussion.

WORKING WITH MULTIPLE STIMULI IN THE GROUP

One of the most common questions that arises at focus group seminars or at client meetings is how many different stimuli can effectively be used in a focus group. Normally, this subject arises when a client is seeking to evaluate consumer attitudes toward a series of different advertising, promotional, or packaging concepts, although it also can occur when the client is seeking to identify the most effective positioning for a product, service, or institution.

Although there is no definitive answer to this question, a few key guidelines will help both the moderator and the client arrive at the "right" number of ideas to test in the group. Specifically:

- The more the ideas are really different, the greater number of concepts you can effectively test. Qualitative research can be an excellent vehicle for evaluating the relative preferences of conceptual ideas; however, focus groups or one-on-one interviews cannot be sufficiently precise to discriminate between two very similar ideas. The technique is not intended to provide this level of precision and should not be used to this end.

- The simpler the concepts presented to the group, the more different ideas can be tested. For example, if the research is intended to obtain reactions to a one- or two-line description of a product or service as a screening device for future work, then it is possible to do a great number of these (i.e., 10-15) very effectively in a 2-hour focus group. On the other hand, if the product or service descriptions are very detailed, it may not be possible to effectively evaluate more than two or three in a group situation.

- Finally, there is some correlation between the level of formal education of the participants and the number of different concepts that can generally be evaluated. Specifically, the more education group members have, the more concepts they can normally evaluate. This is because people who have gone through many years of formal education are accustomed to reading problems and providing solutions in writing and therefore are less intimidated by the process than people who have had very little formal education.

Another frequently raised question related to working with multiple stimuli concerns the most effective way to show several different ideas to a focus group so that each of them is not affected by the ones that have been shown before. Although there is no way to ensure that no biases are developed as the participants move through the various concepts, we have found that some actions can be taken to dramatically reduce the likelihood that bias will be produced and be detrimental to the overall research effort.

First, *the order in which concepts are presented should be rotated from one group to the next,* so that the same idea is not always shown first, second, third, or last. This is an obvious solution that definitely will help reduce the effect of a possible order bias on participants' reactions to external stimuli.

Second, *the concepts should be presented individually but sequentially, with respondents writing comments but engaging in no discussion between the ideas.* The rationale for this approach is that participants need to be exposed to one idea at a time and then to provide a brief written reaction to the concept shown before moving to the next concept. Experience has shown that if you present an idea and then discuss reactions to it before showing the group the next concept, the people in the group will become increasingly more articulate and judgmental as the presentations continue. In effect, they will try to provide responses to the later concepts that incorporate the reactions of others in the groups, trying in this way to make themselves sound more knowledgeable throughout the process.

This approach to presenting concepts to focus groups is not universally accepted within the research community: Some moderators and other marketing professionals would rather discuss each idea individually and set it aside before moving on to the next. They believe that the depth of information generated is richer and that this method permits the individual to provide a clear point of view about each of the ideas.

Further, these researchers feel that presenting multiple concepts to participants sequentially results in information overload and confusion among the participants.

It has been my experience over the past 20 years that presenting concepts individually but sequentially *without* any discussion between them will generate much better inputs overall and is the best way to use external stimuli in a focus group. The only exception to this rule is when the information contained in each concept presentation is long and/or very complex and therefore requires the participant to spend a considerable time reading and understanding the idea before evaluating it. In this type of scenario, we present one concept at a time and then seek to encourage the group to discuss each before moving on to the next. This is because the complex nature of the idea reduces the likelihood that most people will be able to keep the information straight between concepts, and this in turn reduces the quality of the discussion about each.

Third, in dealing with multiple concepts, *the important principle is to use an exercise that will polarize the people in the groups relative to the various ideas before the discussion commences.* This is a very helpful way to determine which of the ideas presented generate the most positive and the most negative reactions in a way that will facilitate the group discussion about them. The following will provide an example of how to use this technique for a situation in which a group has been exposed to a series of different ad concepts. The same approach can be used for almost any presentation of multiple stimuli.

A group is shown four different advertising executions with the goal of identifying an advertising approach (i.e., visual and headline idea) to which the target audience can relate well. After presenting each of the concepts to the group and asking them to write down specific reactions to each, the moderator asks them to identify the execution to which they relate the most and the one to which they relate the least.

Then the moderator obtains a tally from the group as to how many people felt each of the concepts was the most and how many felt each of them was the least easy to relate to. In most circumstances, one or two of the four ideas will stand out as being best received or worst received by the bulk of the people in the focus group. This can be an excellent starting point for the discussion, as the moderator can say to the group that "six of the 10 of you found the 'X' concept to be the one they related to best, and two of the people in the room found it to be the one they related to the least. Now let's hear the feelings from each side about why they responded as they did, and let's see if they can convince the people with the other opinion to change their mind." This will become a very productive discussion about the "X" concept. When that discussion is exhausted, the moderator goes to the next one that had the greatest differentiation in the room and facilitates a similar discussion. This same approach should be used to go through all the ideas until the moderator feels that the group inputs are no longer adding substance to the discussion.

TWO EFFECTIVE SUMMARY EXERCISES WHEN WORKING WITH MULTIPLE EXTERNAL STIMULI

When the discussion of the various stimuli has been completed and the moderator feels that he or she has elicited as much as possible from the participants, two additional exercises can be used that often will add still more useful information on the topic under consideration. A brief description of each follows.

Combining Inputs

One useful exercise is to have the participants in the room look at all the stimuli to which they were exposed (e.g., the four advertising examples described above) and try to develop one more concept, with the restriction that they must use only elements from the existing four to create the new one. For example, they might take part of the visual from one and add in the headline from another along with the subcopy of a third. This is a very helpful exercise, as it often will reveal which visuals and ideas are the strongest out of all the stimuli to which participants were exposed. By combining elements of them into a new concept, we can learn what is important to the participants and apply this learning to further development of the concept. In executing this exercise, it is often a good idea to have everyone in the group begin with the same concept and then add and subtract from that one to come up with their new "collage."

Cub Art Director/Copywriter

Another excellent summary exercise that often will generate some important new insights involves asking the participants to take 5 to 10 minutes to write a headline idea along with a drawing or description of a visual that would represent the most effective way to present this concept. The goal is to get each of the people to develop his or her sense of how to communicate the idea most effectively. The output from this exercise can generate some creative insights that can be used by the client organization as input for further creative development efforts. This type of exercise must be explained very carefully to the client observers in the back room, particularly if any creative personnel in attendance might have a vested interest in the reactions to any of the concepts or ideas that have been presented. These people should be told that the purpose of this exercise is to elicit reactions from the participants concerning the elements of the material to which they were exposed that were most meaningful to them. It is essential that the moderator explain that he or she is not using the energies of the group to try to do the agency job of creative writing. This is only an exercise to generate inputs that can be used by the professionals to improve on the quality of the outputs that have already been generated.

COMMON MISTAKES IN DEVELOPING AND USING EXTERNAL STIMULI IN FOCUS GROUPS AND HOW THEY CAN BE AVOIDED

The balance of this chapter will identify the most common mistakes that are made when external stimuli are used in focus groups. All of them can be avoided if the people involved in the research process have a complete going-in understanding of the overall importance of external stimuli to the total focus group process and the principal guidelines for using stimuli in group sessions. The most frequent mistakes I have seen in this context are:

1. *The participants do not understand the idea that is presented.* This is probably the most common problem that moderators face when dealing with written stimuli such as concept statements, new

product descriptions, or positioning ideas. The idea is presented to the participants, but the people in the group are not able to provide a thoughtful response to the concept because they did not understand the content. This is a function of one of the following factors:

- The description of the concept may be poorly written in that it is complicated and difficult to understand or does not anticipate the questions of readers by providing all the information they need to make a judgment. Often concepts are described in highly technical terms in order to satisfy internal corporate needs, but this level of technicality is not appropriate for use in a focus group environment.
- The participants are the wrong target for this concept as currently written. It is often necessary to write a concept statement differently for various target segments, due to their age, education level, job function, or understanding of the basic product or service area.

2. *The participants do not believe any of the claims made in the statement and therefore do not know how to react to the information.* This also is a very common situation in presenting new product concepts, particularly if the description presents some performance data that seem too good to be true to the participants. In this situation, it is essential that the moderator present the concepts by telling the participants that their reaction must be based on the assumption that everything in the statement is true. At the same time, the moderator should tell the participants to make notes next to all the statements they do not believe, as these will be covered in a separate part of the discussion.

3. *The concept is universally rejected by the groups.* This can occur under one of the following situations:

- The idea may be very bad, and the client organization has not been able to look at the concept objectively. Sometimes it is very difficult for the individual who develops a concept to think it could be anything but fantastic. As discouraging as this may be at the time of the focus groups, it is important to learn, and it is far better to learn it at this stage of product development than further down the road.
- The concept may be written so badly that it emphasizes the wrong benefits of the product or service and therefore is rejected outright.

In summary, the use of external stimuli to elicit reactions from participants in focus groups is one of the most effective ways to encourage in-depth interactions and discussions about topics of interest. However, if a moderator is to use this capability effectively, sufficient time and energy must be put into the development of the stimuli to be used so that they are of maximum value in light of the objectives of the research effort. The better the quality of the stimuli, the better will be the output from the focus groups in which they are employed. Further, the moderator must be very careful about how the various external stimuli are presented to the participants in order to ensure that a bias is not developed on the basis of the presentation of the ideas.

11

THE MODERATOR REPORT

The end product of focus groups is generally a report that is written by the moderator to provide the client organization with a summary of findings, conclusions, and recommendations from the research project. The report is an important tool for clients to use in planning the next steps of the project; it also serves as a historical record of the results of the research. This chapter will discuss the format of a typical report and how it should be developed and presented to the client organization. It will also outline some key issues that frequently arise when a report is written for an intermediary between the moderator and the ultimate client, such as a market research department, an advertising agency, or an independent consultant.

THE IMPORTANCE OF A WRITTEN REPORT

Some client organizations try to save money by not including a written report as part of the focus group project. Typically, they make this decision when they are constrained by a very tight budget and must try to cut out all unnecessary expenses of the research. If all of their decision makers plan to attend all of the focus groups, they may feel that they do not need to pay an outsider for a report. Often they commission someone else to do the report, such as an employee of the client organization or a consultant or advertising agency that they already have under retainer, so that a report can be generated without incurring additional costs. But no matter what the cost restraints are, I feel it is always a mistake to eliminate the formal report from a focus group project if you retain an experienced moderator to work with your organization.

It is essential that a report be written for all focus group projects because the report is the formal record of the focus groups, to which employees can refer in the future as issues arise that might be addressed by consulting the focus group output. Although most focus groups also have tapes (video and/or audio) of the proceedings, we find that it is very unusual for an organization to watch or listen to the tapes after the groups are completed. Further, without a report, it is almost impossible to get people in the organization to agree on what really happened in the groups and what the implications were for the actions that resulted from the recommendations. Most people seem to have selective memory and therefore will recall what they want to remember from the groups, and this may not be representative of all the facts.

It is essential that the report be written by the moderator rather than an employee or outside consultant. Although this does not preclude the development of a separate report by one of these entities, the moderator report should be the "official document" from the focus groups. If a client does not request a moderator report, they are not receiving some of the most important added value benefits that the moderator brings to the assignment. Specifically, these include

- Experience in interpreting the findings from the group.
- Objectivity in both the interpretation of the findings and the development of conclusions and recommendations. An experienced moderator will not let corporate preferences (or politics) get in the way of the report and will provide conclusions and recommendations that are based on the group inputs rather than a response to what the client might wish to hear.

- Speed of preparation of the report. Because the report is normally the final part of an assignment and will result in billings to the client, there is a strong incentive for the moderator to get the report completed as quickly as possible. This generally will happen much faster than it would if the report were being done by a corporate employee or an outside consultant.

A key issue in this regard, and one that is somewhat controversial in the focus group industry, is the real authorship of a report within a focus group research organization. A large percentage of moderators will use project personnel to write the reports on the basis of tapes and/or notes prepared by the moderator or a note taker sitting in the back room. Although this is a very common practice, most clients do not know about it and assume that their moderator writes the entire report.

I am very much against the practice of using others to write the report for the moderator, even if the document is reviewed and modified by the moderator before going to the client organization. Clients deserve the full attention of the moderator throughout the project, starting with in-depth involvement in defining the background, objectives, and planned execution of the research and culminating with an interpretation of the findings and their implications. Clients should not accept focus group reports that are not written entirely by the moderator.

TYPES OF REPORTS

There is no standard formula for a moderator report in the focus group industry. However, generally three types of reports are used.

Formal Report

The most common type of report is a full, formal document that summarizes the key facts from the research and contains detailed conclusions and recommendations. Most clients expect this type of document to come out of focus groups.

The biggest difference in the way formal reports are written by different moderators is whether they contain verbatim comments from the participants. Some moderators feel it is important to include direct quotations to support the observations they make in the text, as they believe it adds "texture" to the document. Other moderators do not believe in using verbatims in focus group reports, as it is almost always possible to find a statement to support any point that the moderator wants to emphasize in the report. Further, many moderators believe that the use of verbatims makes the report too focused on micro rather than macro issues and that the methodology is much more effective when addressing topics from a more strategic, macro perspective. These moderators would also argue that use of verbatims can put too much importance on the comment from one individual in a series of groups, thus perhaps minimizing the contribution of all the others.

It would not be unusual for a formal report coming out of a focus group series to be 30 or 50 pages long. Later in this chapter, we will provide a suggested outline for the contents of a formal moderator report.

Top-Line Report

Some clients do not want to read an extensive report and ask their moderators to develop a brief (three- to five-page) top line. This document is intended to briefly provide the background for the groups, summarize the most essential findings, and focus on the conclusions and recommendations.

Some client organizations request both top-line and formal reports, but normally only when the moderator has a history of taking a long time to complete the formal report. As a result, the organization uses the top line as the action document and the formal report as the historical record of the proceedings.

Oral/Stand-up Presentations

Many clients prefer to complete a focus group series with a formal presentation in which the moderator presents the key findings from the research and conclusions and recommendations. This is normally requested as a relatively efficient way to involve several different people in the client organization in the research so that everyone can hear the moderator's comments at the same time and then discuss the implications of the focus groups for the future. Often clients will ask for a stand-up presentation and a formal report because they use the report as the historical record and the stand-up presentation as a way to generate actions.

THE FORMAT FOR A FORMAL MODERATOR REPORT

This section will provide a suggested format for a moderator report. I have used this format for many years and have found that it generates a high level of consumer acceptance. Almost all reports that are written by me or any of the moderators at Groups Plus, Inc., follow the format that is shown below.

Introduction

This is a very brief section that summarizes the dates and timing of the focus groups and provides a succinct statement of the objective of the research and the anticipated use of the results by the client organization. In addition, this section normally will provide a summary of the sections of the report so that the reader will understand how the document is organized and what can be expected in each part.

Caveat

I believe that all focus group reports should contain a brief caveat that identifies the limitations of qualitative research so that the uninformed reader will have a framework in which to put the information that follows. Table 11.1 shows a typical caveat statement that we include in all focus group reports.

Methodology

This is a relatively brief section that is intended to summarize the key details regarding how the research was conducted, as well as important administrative information that could be germane to a full understand-

Table 11.1   Caveat

It should be noted that the focus group methodology is qualitative and exploratory in nature and is not intended to provide data that are projectable to a stated universe. Focus groups are designed to elicit reactions from participants about a particular topic and to generate ideas and concepts that will help the client to understand a subject area. The output from focus groups also is often helpful in developing hypotheses and parameters to be included in a quantitative study.

Never should the results from focus group research be considered representative of any population segment or a point of view of a specific target universe. The nonrandom method of recruitment and the small size of the sample do not permit this type of observation.

Nevertheless, the results of a well-designed and properly conducted focus group can provide a great deal of marketing insight and direction and should be used accordingly.

---

ing of the report. Specifically, this section should include statements that cover at least the following topics:

- The number of groups that were included in the series and the markets where they were held
- The approach to recruiting, in terms of how the participants were identified (lists, facility data bank, advertising, referrals, etc.), how many people were recruited for each group, and the number who actually participated
- The composition of the various groups, which would normally involve summarizing the most important recruitment criteria that were used in the selection process
- The honorarium that was paid to the participants
- A summary of the flow of the discussion in the groups, which will give the reader a sense of how the moderator conducted the sessions
- A description of any "external stimuli" that were used in the groups as a tool to elicit comments from the participants
- An indication as to whether the groups were taped and what was done with the tapes at the conclusion of the sessions
- A summary of the client-related personnel who observed the sessions from behind the mirror so that there is a historical record of who actually watched the groups

- An indication of the approximate length of the groups and who did the moderating

Findings

The findings section is intended to be a summary of the most important "facts" that emerged from the discussion. I have found that the most effective way to organize this section is to use the order of information outlined in the moderator guide. Although every point in the guide will not be reflected in the findings section, and although normally some topics will be included that are not in the guide, this is a logical way to set up the section if it can be assumed that the guide was well designed at the outset.

We have also found that the actual writing of this section is most effective when one topic is handled on a page at a time, in a format of first a headline idea that represents the key observation about the particular topic area and then subpoints on the same page that add substance to the main point that has been developed. Although this format results in a report that is often longer (in terms of pages) than a traditional approach, it has been our experience that clients find this a useful way to receive the information, as it is easy to read, understand, and digest the material from the groups.

Conclusions and Recommendations

These are two separate sections, but they are discussed together here because many people have difficulty developing these elements of the focus group report. Specifically, over the years we have found that many people have trouble differentiating among findings, conclusions, and recommendations. For example:

- A *finding* is a fact or piece of information that emerged from the group discussion. There are no moderator judgments or interpretations in a finding. In general, both the client and moderator will be in agreement relative to the findings because these are simply reporting what was said in the groups.
- A *conclusion* is the interpretation of the findings in terms of the objectives of the research effort. For example, a finding might be that

the participants did not like the new soft drink concept that was presented, whereas the conclusion would be that the concept does not seem to represent a viable business opportunity for the client at the present time. The conclusions and recommendations section can contain many different conclusions, but all must have some relationship to the findings and be focused on the overall objectives of the research effort. In terms of format, we find that the best way to present conclusions is to make a one-sentence statement of the conclusion and then provide a transition to numerous support points from the findings that support the conclusion. This enables the reader to understand how the moderator arrived at the conclusion that was developed.

- The *recommendations* are the specific action steps that the moderator believes the client organization should take next in light of the conclusions that have been developed. For example, using the soft drink concept as an example, perhaps the moderator would recommend a different way to position the product, a different target audience, or a different flavor, container, or name in order to stimulate interest in the idea. Also the moderator might recommend that additional research be implemented once the concept has been revised so that the new idea can be validated.

Appendix

The appendix is an important part of the report in that it provides a record of the details of the group implementation. The appendix is the section of a focus group report in which the moderator should include documents such as the recruitment screening questionnaire, the discussion guide, and copies of any materials ("external stimuli") that were used during the groups. This is very important because they provide a future reader of the report with the background necessary to understand the recruiting approach, the details covered in the discussion, and the specific stimuli to which the participants were exposed.

THE ISSUE OF REPORT INTEGRITY

One of the issues that moderators will occasionally face is that a low-level client person or intermediary (i.e., consultant, ad agency) will want to be able to influence the content of the moderator report, either before it is written or after it has been prepared and sent to the client. Although this is not common, it presents a significant dilemma to most moderators because the objectivity they bring to an assignment is one of the most important reasons they exist.

How is a moderator to deal with a direct client contact who insists on changing some of the findings, conclusions, or recommendations of the report? The answer to this depends on the following factors:

1. *The nature of the changes that are requested.* If the client contact points out factual errors in the findings section that the moderator agrees are mistakes, it is appropriate for the moderator to change the report to reflect reality. However, if the client contact does not agree with the way the moderator has interpreted the findings in developing the conclusions, then the moderator should ensure that he or she is comfortable with the judgments made and, if so, not change things to make the client happy.

2. *The motivation of the client contact.* I have had situations in which a client wanted me to soften the intensity of my conclusions and recommendations because it would make senior management unhappy with the outcome of the groups (in terms of the reactions to a product or program the company has launched). In this type of situation, I would never change the report, as my integrity as a moderator is more important than the business that might be generated by the client contact's feeling that I would change aspects of the work to make them look better.

It has been my experience that the most effective way to deal with requests to change reports or disagreements on conclusions or recommendations between the moderator and the client is by agreeing to disagree. Specifically, I suggest that my direct client contact send my report forward to their management with a cover note that indicates the points of disagreement. This gives management a chance to benefit from the perspective of the moderator, while at the same time giving the people in the company the opportunity to disagree with aspects of the report. It has been my experience that almost all senior managers are very much against being shielded from facts or unpleasantness, as this can get everyone into trouble over time. It is better to present the information as it is identified, even if very negative, so that appropriate plans can be made to implement changes that will enable the company to address the problems that occur.

RECOMMENDING MORE RESEARCH
IN MODERATOR REPORTS

It is not unusual for a key conclusion from a focus group series to suggest the need for additional research. However, moderators should be very careful about recommendations that might seem to represent a pitch for more business from the client organization. This is not to suggest that a moderator should not draw this type of conclusion (and make a subsequent recommendation) but rather that the wording should be stated carefully so the recommendation does not appear to be self-serving.

SUMMARY

One should not underestimate the importance of the moderator report in the overall spectrum of focus group variables. For many people in client organizations, such a report is the only way they ever get to see the output of the moderator and is likely to be the document that lives long after the focus groups are forgotten. As a result, moderators should be willing to allocate enough time and energy to the report so that it reflects the best possible thinking they can bring to the assignment, for it will serve as a lasting example of their work.

12

MODERATING FUNDAMENTALS

This chapter covers the essential guidelines that moderators will need to understand and master if they wish to maximize their effectiveness working with groups of people. The topics discussed range from relatively minor behavioral suggestions for how the moderator should act before, during, and after a group session to subjects of major import such as listening skills and methods of framing questions to achieve the best possible output from the research. For many years, I have felt that there is a definite similarity between the principles that make one an effective moderator and those that a golf professional might teach students trying to learn the game. Specifically, getting a good grasp of the *fundamentals* first will make one dramatically more capable of executing the advanced elements when these are attempted.

THE MODERATOR PERSONA

Chapter 4 discussed the various reasons the focus group technique works so effectively, and it emphasized the role that the moderator should play in the process. Essentially, the moderator must be the orchestra leader in the group, directing the flow of the discussion, but at the same time he or she must also be the authority figure in the room who is able to build rapport with the participants so that they want to cooperate in order to achieve the objectives of the research. For the moderator to fill this dual role, some important principles must be understood. These key guidelines are summarized below.

How the Moderator Should Be Dressed

There are many different views regarding the importance of the moderator's appearance, and even more regarding what is appropriate for this person to wear in a focus group environment. It is my strong opinion that the general guidelines for the moderator's appearance should include

- Being comfortable
- Not appearing flashy
- Not dressing up so much as to intimidate the participants
- Not dressing down so much as to appear not to have authority

Specifically, a female moderator who comes into the room dressed like someone out of a Saks Fifth Avenue catalog may have great difficulty relating to the people with whom she is working. Similarly, the same woman who shows up in jeans and sneakers probably will have difficulty obtaining the respect of the participants, as they will probably find her to be less than professional in her appearance.

Some male moderators feel they must be very dressed up, wearing suits and ties, in order to gain the respect of the group. Others feel it is important to dress down as much as possible to communicate that they are not from the corporate world but rather represent the research community. In my opinion, neither is on target and will work to the ultimate benefit of the moderator.

The most appropriate dress for a moderator, whether male or female, is what is generally known today as business casual. For men, a sport coat or sweater without a tie is very appropriate for virtually any group, and for women, a basic casual outfit with very minimal jewelry will work very effectively. A key objective should be that the moderator's clothes not stand out in any way and definitely do not draw attention to him or her.

The Moderator's Demeanor

The moderator should take control of the group immediately, in terms of sending a message to the participants that they must follow the rules that have been established regarding such things as talking with each other, leaving the room, or obtaining refreshments during the group. The following are a few key suggestions that will help the moderator project the most appropriate demeanor in the room.

The moderator should *not* enter the group room until all the participants are seated and ready to start the discussion. Some moderators will stand at the door and greet the people as they come in, and others will be in the room when the participants arrive so they can welcome them to the session. It is my strong belief that a moderator is best served by not doing either of these things, as they create an impression that the moderator is one of the group rather than the person who is leading the session. It is preferable for the moderator to come into the room, get the immediate attention of the participants, and begin providing direction/instruction relative to the activities that will be occurring. This quickly sends a message to the group that the moderator is in control.

First names should be used on name tags for all groups because this creates an informal atmosphere in the room that encourages people to share their views about a topic being discussed. First names should be used regardless of the age, title, or profession of the respondents. Some moderators will use "Dr." for medical groups or "Mr./Ms." for groups with persons who are considerably older than they are, but in both situations the absence of first names puts the participants in a superior psychological position to the moderator, who has a name tag showing a first name only.

At the start of the group, it is important for the moderator to be very clear with the participants regarding the "rules" that have been established for the discussion. This would include such things as

- The importance of having only one person speaking at a time

- The need to speak loudly so that the speaker can be heard and the voice captured by the tapes
- Whether the people are encouraged to get food or drink during the sessions
- Rules on beepers and cell phones

It is also important for the moderator to communicate to the participants in a firm (but friendly) way at the beginning of the group that they are to follow the directions of the moderator regarding the rules of the group. Although this may seem very obvious to some, one of the major reasons that focus groups get out of control and do not achieve their objectives is that the participants take control of the discussion and lead it where they want it to go. Some moderators have difficulty inserting themselves into the discussion and becoming the police officer or orchestra director with the mission of directing the focus of the discussion to ensure that it is consistent with the needs of the client organization.

During the group, it may be necessary for the moderator to reassert his or her authority in the room by indicating to specific people that they are not following the rules, such as letting only one person talk at a time or not leaving the room to make phone calls or visit the restroom. By taking this approach, the moderator will be able to retain much more effective control over the actions of the participants, and the group will run more effectively.

INTRODUCING THE TAPING WITHOUT
HAVING IT AFFECT THE GROUP DISCUSSION

Most moderators feel it is their ethical responsibility to tell participants in a focus group that they are being audiotaped and/or videotaped or, in the case of a videoconferenced group, that the session is being transmitted live to "X" locations where people are watching. If these elements are handled properly by the moderator, the participants will soon forget about them, and their existence will have no impact on the willingness of the individuals to share their views about the topics being discussed. But if the moderator attempts to conceal these elements, it is likely that they will be a significant distraction, as the participants will wonder why they have not been informed about them.

The most effective way to address and then dismiss the taping is for the moderator to mention its existence very early in the group, when the basic instructions and administrative details are being covered. Further, if the moderator talks about these elements in a low-key, matter-of-fact way and does not draw attention to them again, it is a virtual certainty that they will not become a distraction to the group.

NAMES AND NAME TAGS

As indicated several different places in this book, an important part of the group dynamics is the atmosphere that is created in the room and the relationship that is established between the moderator and the participants. One issue that can affect this is the way names are used in a focus group. First and most important is the assurance that each person in the group has a name tag so that the moderator and the participants (and those who are observing from behind the one-way mirror) do not have to remember each person's name throughout the session. Further, having name tags makes the environment more friendly, as it facilitates conversation among the people in the group. I have always found that the best name tag is a tent card placed on the table with the individual's name written as large as possible on both sides of the card. This is to enable the moderator to see the name both when sitting down and when walking around the room to use an easel, to show a concept using the chair rail, or for any other reason.

The name displayed on the name tag also can be important to the way a focus group dynamic plays out. Most focus group facilities make up name tags in advance to facilitate the sign-in process when participants come to the groups. The name on the tag is therefore the name that the recruiter put on the screener when the individual agreed to participate in the groups. However, in many cases, this is not the name the participant wishes to be called in a social setting. For example, Michael might prefer to be called Mike, Anthony to be called Tony, and Michelle to be called Shelly. If the preferred name is not used on the tag, then the moderator and the others will either have to remember what the person wants to be called or be willing to use a name that is not as comfortable for the participant as would be ideal.

Because of the preference of so many people for nicknames or short-ened versions of their given name, it is useful to provide instructions to the focus group facility to make up the name tags when the participants arrive so they can ask participants what they prefer to be called rather than to assume that the name on the screener is correct.

USING NAMES IN MEDICAL GROUPS

A unique situation with regard to the naming conventions for focus groups occurs when research is being conducted with medical person-nel or others with formal titles (e.g., military, academic). Most focus group moderators will use the formal title (e.g., Dr. Smith) on the name tag for the participants and yet be very comfortable with their own name tag saying Sally or Sam. This is *not* the recommended approach, as it can affect the dynamics of the group and the role of the moderator in the room by making the moderator appear less in control of the session. Therefore, I have found it beneficial to indicate to the "titled" individu-als when they arrive at the focus group facility that we will be using first names today and then to ask what they would like to be called. In the rare case that a titled person objects to this convention, I will not permit him or her to participate in the group, as it would set him or her apart from the others in the room.

This same convention applies to moderators who prefer to use titles or more formal name designators (e.g., Mr. Parker, Ms. Shepherd). Al-though this may feel comfortable for the moderator, it generally will have a negative effect on the ability of the individual to develop immedi-ate rapport with the participants.

THE ROLE OF LISTENING IN EFFECTIVE
FOCUS GROUP MODERATION

Listening skills are an essential ingredient for an effective and an effi-cient career as a focus group moderator. If a moderator is unable to re-member what a participant said earlier in a session, it will be difficult to integrate that information with the inputs provided by this individual later in the group. Further, if a moderator must always listen to the focus group tapes following a group to get the essential inputs from the groups, the amount of time he or she will have to spend on each focus group project will be dramatically increased. Therefore, it is essential that a moderator make a commitment to develop good listening skills and to use tools that will aid in the recall of key information that emerges from the group discussion.

Books and seminars are available to help people improve their ability to listen to others, and the basic premise of these is that listening skills can be learned. The following will provide some suggestions that might help focus group moderators to improve their listening skills.

- *Make active listening a conscious effort.* If you are aware of the importance of improving your listening skills and make this a personal objective, your heightened awareness will be an important first step in the process.
- *Focus your efforts in the room on listening rather than talking.* Some focus group moderators feel they must entertain their clients in the back room and therefore feel they must find any opportunity they can to say something clever. Other moderators believe they must constantly be explaining things to the group or providing detailed direction to the participants for the group discussion to accomplish the objectives. When a moderator is talking, he or she is not listening, so the more talking, the less listening. The solution is to be conscious of the amount of conversation that comes from the moderator and to try to minimize this as much as possible so that there is more time to focus on the information generated from the participants.
- *Be intimately familiar with the content of the discussion guide and the objectives of the groups.* One thing that will seriously inhibit the listening skills of a moderator is the need for this individual to be planning what topics will be covered next in the group. This need will take away from the moderator's concentration on what is happening in the room, as he or she will be focusing more on what to do next with the group than on what is happening at that moment.
- *Conduct the group as if there were no audiotapes or videotapes to refer to afterwards.* Some moderators feel that they do not have to pay close attention to what is happening in the room because they have the

tapes (or a note taker in the back room) to fall back on if they need additional information. However, with this crutch, some people will reduce their listening efforts, and this can hurt the appropriateness of the follow-up probing, as well as the final analysis of findings. If moderators work under the premise that they do not have these backups, they will be much more likely to focus more on listening to the participants.

- *Practice "in and out" listening during the group.* This is a technique aimed at enabling individuals to clear their mind of other thoughts so that they can focus on the present situation. For example, if you are conducting a group and have a topic that you realize must be covered later, the best idea is to quickly write yourself a note about it as soon as you think of it, in a place that you allocate to this type of information. By writing it down (and particularly in a special place that you can refer to later), you clear your mind of this thought and are much better equipped to listen to what is happening in the group. This same technique should be applied to inputs you get from participants that you feel are likely to be important. By writing them down quickly in a shorthand form that you develop for yourself, you can capture the information and then return to the active listening in the room.

- *Take short but specific notes during the group using a group diagram* —that is, a form (see Figure 12.1) that identifies the position in the room of each of the participants. At the beginning of the group when the people are introduced, the moderator indicates who is at each place. Then, during the session, there is a specific place for writing brief notes about the inputs of the individuals, which can be referred to later. By focusing on this type of input, moderators will force themselves to listen better to ensure that they get the inputs, while also using the "in and out" listening skills to capture the thought but getting back to the content of the group with virtually no lost time.

- *Focus on making eye contact with each participant when he or she is talking.* This will help you to remember what has been said by this individual, as the eye contact forces you to focus specifically on the person talking.

- *Use the discussion guide as a vehicle for note taking.* In addition to the seating chart, which is helpful to keep track of specific items men-

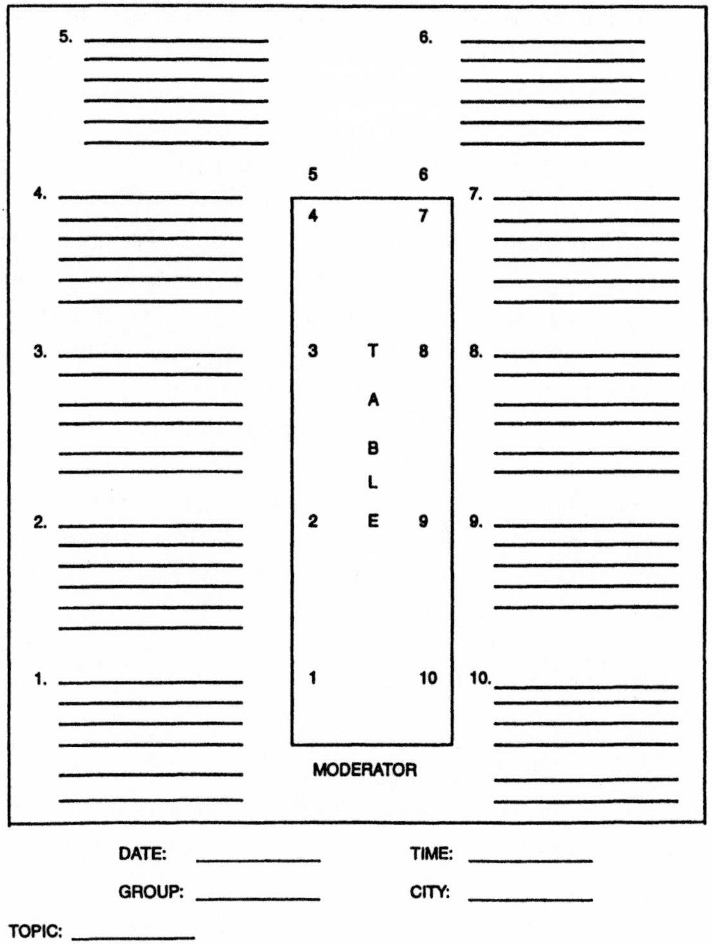

Figure 12.1. Focus Group Research Respondent Comment Record

tioned by individuals in the room, it is helpful to use the moderator guide for notes taken during the group. The value of using the guide for this purpose is that you can jot down group reactions about particular topics being discussed next to the item indicated on the discussion guide. This can be very helpful after the group series is completed, as it will enable you to go back to the discussion guide for each session and identify the most important information that you wrote down on a topic-by-topic basis.

USING POINT SCALES TO HELP
FACILITATE GROUP INTERACTION

Focus groups are qualitative research, so there is no place in this methodology for trying to quantify the participant inputs. If the client organization is seeking quantitative data, then it would be prudent to consider the many quantitative research methodologies as options that will achieve the goals of generating data from the study.

On the other hand, quantitative approaches in focus group moderation can have a very useful role in stimulating participants to think carefully about what they are saying and to assist the moderator in encouraging discussion among the people in the group. Two examples of how quantitative scales can be extremely helpful to the focus group process are described below.

Idea Assessment/Personal Reaction

It is quite common during a focus group for the moderator to ask the participants to react to an idea, some type of external stimulus, or even their own capabilities regarding a particular task (e.g., computer literacy, growing plants, organizing household records). In these types of situations, it is often helpful to use a numerical scale as the benchmark against which the people provide their assessment and then to ensure that the participants can explain the rationale behind the rating they provide.

For example, if the moderator is seeking to understand how the participants in the group feel about a new product idea, it is often helpful to use a 10-point scale (which is placed on an easel for easy reference by the participants and which has at least the endpoints and the middle of the scale identified as to the meaning of the numbers) to have the people identify their feelings. A rating of 9 might suggest a very high level of interest about the idea, whereas a 3 might show a very low level of interest. To arrive at a number, participants have to really think about the idea that was presented and be able to provide a relative judgment as to how they feel this new concept would work for them. Participants provide a specific representation of their feelings (i.e., the number indicated) and then are expected to explain the basis for this thinking. As will be discussed in a later chapter, there are some strong advantages to obtaining this information in writing, but this is not essential, nor is it relevant to the discussion of the technique in this chapter.

This technique also can be helpful when more than one idea is presented to the participants for this type of rating, as it can be used as a stimulus for comparing ideas. For example, if the participant gave a rating of 6 to one product and 9 to the other, the moderator can use this difference as an easy way to begin a "compare-and-contrast" discussion about the differences between the two items being reviewed.

Group Polarization

One of the most important uses of numbers in a focus group situation is to identify where the various people in the room stand on a particular issue, as this is valuable to the moderator in stimulating group discussion. To give an example of how this would be used, we will assume that a new product concept has been presented to a focus group. It is helpful to have participants write down their reactions to the new concept, using both a point scale (I use a 10-point "smiley" scale; see Figure 12.2) to indicate how they feel about the idea and a brief description indicating the reasons why they feel the way they do about the concept. Once this information is obtained, it is helpful to ask each of the participants in the room for his or her numerical rating before any discussion commences. This is where the number scale helps the moderator polarize the groups, as the expression of the numbers will identify where the various people stand on the issue in question. For example, if there are 10 people in the group and two provide a rating of 3, four provide a rating of 6, one provides a rating of 8, and the other three provide a rating of 9 or 10, the moderator is in a position to ask the people to talk to each other about why they responded as they did. It is generally helpful to begin with the people on the poles (i.e., either the 3s or the 9/10s) by asking them why they felt the way they did about the idea that generated the rating. After the people on one side of the issue explain their views, it is useful to ask the people who feel oppositely about the idea to talk to their peers and explain why they feel the way they do. This will normally stimulate good discussion

Figure 12.2. A 10-Point "Smiley" Scale

between the people with the differing views and should elicit rich inputs regarding the strengths and limitations of the concept. The people in the group who fall in the middle of the two poles can be brought into the discussion by asking which of the others (at the poles) share views that are most similar to those expressed by them and what it would take to increase their overall interest in the idea.

The purpose of this polarization is to stimulate discussion among the participants in order to uncover the reasons for the differences in opinions. But in some circumstances, there will not be much difference between the views, as all the people will either like or dislike the idea and will thus provide essentially the same rating. In this type of scenario, the moderator can use the number ratings to ask the group why they felt so negative or positive about the concept and what were the major elements of the concept that stimulated the reaction. Similarly, if the participants provide a very lukewarm response (i.e., ratings of 6, 7, and 8), the moderator can use the number system to ask the various participants what it would take to increase their rating to a 9 or 10. Often, this approach will result in the participants' identifying the key missing ingredient(s) that would produce a more positive response.

FRAMING QUESTIONS TO ASK THE GROUP

In an earlier chapter, we discussed the importance of the role of the moderator and the need for this individual to maintain some distance from the participants. Another key aspect of successful moderating is to communicate to the participants that the moderator has absolutely no stake in the outcome of the groups and that the answers provided by the people in the room do not have any impact on the moderator. Because of the authoritative role of the moderator, the approach taken to elicit responses from the group can have a dramatic impact on the degree to which the participants provide answers that really represent their own views, as opposed to saying what they feel the moderator (or others in the room) want to hear. Therefore, the way questions are asked and follow-up probes are employed is vital to effective focus group moderation. This section will focus on identifying different approaches for eliciting information from the participants that will reflect their views rather than their perception of what others want to hear.

Effective Techniques to Encourage Discussion

Eliciting information from a focus group requires that a moderator provide some type of verbal stimulus that will start a discussion. As a result, the moderator has the opportunity to influence the group if he or she is not aware of some fundamental principles to follow that will help to keep that from happening.

For example, it is essential that the moderator not enter a focus group session with a point of view about the topic being discussed. This is an essential ingredient to having a focus group that is not influenced by the views of the moderator. Although this may seem obvious to some, it is very common for a client to ask the moderator what he or she feels about the particular topic to be covered in the group before the sessions. Experienced moderators will train themselves to avoid forming a bias in advance of the group, in recognition that this will affect their ability to present a neutral attitude to the participants.

The way questions are framed also can significantly affect the response that the moderator will get from the participants. This is due to both the wording of the inquiry/question and the tone of voice that the moderator uses when asking the question.

Tone of Voice

The same moderator response to a participant can have several completely different meanings depending on whether it is framed as a question, a declarative statement, or an exclamation. For example, the following are three possible ways a moderator might respond to a participant who was asked to react to a specific feature presented in a new product concept statement:

- *You don't feel this is an important product feature.* When stated as a declarative sentence, this response is a way the moderator can ensure that he or she has properly paraphrased the response provided by the participants, with no personal bias injected into the response. What it says to the participant is that the moderator understands the communication that has been provided.
- *You don't feel this is an important product feature?* When put in the form of a question, this response has another meaning, as it calls for the participant to explain why he or she feels the way he or she does about the particular topic under discussion. It can be an excellent way for the moderator to stimulate additional discussion from the person without saying any more than is necessary.

- *You don't feel this is an important product feature!* When a response is framed in a tone that implies surprise by the moderator (as would be communicated by an exclamatory tone), the participant is likely to feel that the moderator has a personal bias and is opposed to the participant's answer. This puts the participant in a somewhat defensive position, possibly creating the desire to change his or her answer or go to great extremes to justify the rationale.

Wording of the Follow-Up

The moderator also can significantly influence participants' responses by the wording of a follow-up. For example:

- *I can't believe you don't like this product feature.* This type of statement injects a very strong bias into the discussion, as it communicates that the moderator has a going-in bias in favor of the feature. This will discourage others in the group from expressing a negative reaction, as they will not want to be ridiculed in front of the others like the person to whom this response was directed.
- *I don't understand why you don't like this product feature.* This type of response singles out the participant as being different from others, as the emphasis on the *you* suggests that the moderator expected this person to provide a different response.
- *What don't you like about this product feature?* This type of response asks the question in a neutral way, without expressing any type of moderator bias. It acknowledges the participant's view and is worded in such a way as to encourage the participant to explain his or her views further without feeling a need to justify his or her perspective.

Effective Probing/Follow-Up Questions

An experienced focus group moderator will use many techniques that have been used for decades by psychologists and psychiatrists who seek to motivate their patients to give them more information without having to say a lot to obtain it. Some examples of excellent follow-up questions that will almost always be effective in generating more information from a participant are as follows:

- Why do you feel that way?
- Tell me more.
- In what way?
- I don't understand what you are saying.
- Tell me more about your thoughts about . . .

All of the above are effective follow-up questions because they ask the participant for more information about the topic without making any kind of judgment as to how the moderator feels about it. Also, they seek the follow-up comments in a way that shows the moderator is really interested in what the participant has to say about the topic, so the participant will generally feel comfortable about sharing additional information.

DEALING WITH QUESTIONS ASKED TO THE MODERATOR

It is very common in a focus group situation for a participant to feel the need to ask the moderator questions during the discussion. Essentially, these fall into the following two areas: procedural questions and content questions.

Procedural Questions

Procedural questions relate to administrative issues, such as the need to go to the restroom, the need for additional refreshments, or the way the participant is supposed to complete a written exercise that is requested of him or her during the group. These types of questions can be answered directly, although those that relate to completion of a write-down exercise should be handled very carefully. For example, if it is a question of how to complete a part of an exercise, the moderator should explain this to the group, as it could be an issue for several of the participants. However, if it is a request for the moderator to interpret a question that seeks the participant's opinion about a particular issue, then the best course of action is to tell the individual to complete the exercise as best he or she can and that the questions raised will be addressed when everyone has completed their comments.

Content Questions

It is also common for participants to ask questions about the topic being covered that might relate to elements of a concept statement that they do not fully understand or something they feel is missing from the description. Some examples of the types of questions that would fall into this category, based on a concept for a new combination cellular telephone and Internet access computer, might be:

- Will this be sold by a telephone company or a computer firm?
- Is there a discount for the ISP (Internet service provider) fee if you purchase a phone that uses their service, as in the case of AT&T, which has both cellular service and ISP?
- Is it possible to upgrade the speed at which the phone downloads information from the Internet?

In each of these examples, it would be possible for the moderator to provide an answer, assuming that the briefing from the client organization had addressed the questions and provided the correct information to the moderator. However, by answering the question raised, the moderator would not take advantage of the opportunity to understand why the question was asked, which could provide important information about the research. For example:

- The question regarding the primary seller of this device could uncover some feelings by this participant (and perhaps others in the group) about the level of service he or she would expect from a telephone versus a computer vendor and might identify some added value that would result if the item were sold by one versus the other.
- The question regarding the pricing could reflect significant concerns about the cost of the new product in terms of both the purchase of the hardware and the ongoing costs of Internet access. It might suggest that pricing might be a major leverage point that could affect the success of the program, and this would need to be explored fully by the moderator.
- The third question, dealing with possible upgrades, could be expressing (consciously or unconsciously) the participant's concern about the viability of the technology of this new device and

whether it would be sufficiently hi-tech to work effectively in the current cell phone/computer environment.

The examples provided above are discussed only to emphasize the importance that a moderator should place on all questions raised by focus group participants, as these could represent excellent opportunities to explore new areas of concern that could be integral to the overall project.

Another reason why the moderator should not answer these types of questions is that answers could change the perception of the participants concerning the role that the moderator plays in the overall research effort. For example:

- If the moderator appears too knowledgeable about the topic, the participants may be less willing to accept that the moderator really is an independent part of the process who does not have a stake in the outcome of the research.
- An answer also may encourage participants to enter into a technical discussion with the moderator about a relatively unimportant aspect of the idea being discussed, in order to show off to the other participants how smart they are both in general and compared to the moderator.
- Finally, an answer may detract from the group atmosphere and lead to a situation in which one moderator is talking individually to 10 individual people, all of whom want to find answers to particular questions that are of concern to them. This would dramatically reduce the amount of group interaction and thereby result in a lower quality of information coming out of the research.

HOW TO GET MAXIMUM USE OUT OF CONTENT QUESTIONS RELATIVE TO THE RESEARCH OBJECTIVES

There are basically two objectives that a moderator should have when developing an approach to address a question that is asked of a participant. The first is to understand what really is the issue with the person who generated the question, and the second is to determine how important this issue is to the individual who asked the question and the other people in the group. The approach to dealing with the question must be framed with these two objectives in mind. Therefore, I recommend that the moderator use the following approach(es) when faced with this type of situation:

- The immediate response from the moderator should be to ask the person who asked the question, "Why is it important for you to have this answer?" This should stimulate additional discussion that the moderator can use as to probe the real reasons why the question was raised.
- The follow-up to this discussion should be a question from the moderator that seeks to determine how important this particular aspect of the product is to the individual, both in the absolute and compared to the other aspects of the product that were presented in the concept description. This discussion should involve not only the person who asked the question but the other people in the group because the moderator should try to understand how important the issue is to the rest of the group; this might be an area that requires additional discussion, even though it was not anticipated in planning for the groups.

SING GROUP DYNAMICS TO
HELP PROBE AREAS FURTHER

One of the biggest advantages of the focus group methodology is that the spontaneity of the group dynamic makes it possible to probe further into specific areas that emerge from the group discussion. One way to use this resource is to ask people in the group to address their comments to another individual, with the objective of having the two people engage in a brief discussion about the topic that was raised. An example of this might be the reaction to a new Internet shopping service, in which one person feels it is an excellent concept but is very concerned with the inability to actually see and feel the merchandise being purchased, whereas someone else in the group has indicated that he or she likes the concept and is not troubled by the apparent limitations raised by the other participant. By encouraging these two people to talk about their differences, the moderator would make the session less of a question-and-answer group and more of a discussion among the people in the room who are the key targets for the new product or service.

Further, this interaction between the two people can be the vehicle for drawing others into the discussion in order to determine who else in the room may have concerns like those raised by the original participant and how important these concerns are to the overall assessment of the idea. Further, it enables the moderator to find out who does not share these concerns and why they are not a problem for this group of participants. The net effect of this scenario is that the moderator has taken a response from one individual and opened it to the group for discussion so that the entire energy of the 8 to 10 participants in the room can be focused on this subject for a few minutes. This affords the moderator the opportunity to bring up new issues that appear to affect the attitudes of the various people toward the subject.

TECHNIQUES FOR ENCOURAGING FULL GROUP PARTICIPATION

One of the main complaints that people have about the focus group technique is that one or two people in a session tend to dominate while other people in the room add virtually nothing to the overall discussion. This type of complaint suggests that the moderator conducting the group at issue does not have sufficient experience or training to avoid this type of situation. In a well-planned and well-moderated focus group, all the participants in the room will be very involved in the discussion and feel that they are equal participants in the group with the others. The following will provide some tools and techniques that a moderator can use to dramatically increase the probability that the people in the room will become effective focus group participants.

Using Articulation Questions in the Screening Process

It is helpful to incorporate an articulation question into a recruitment screener, as this can help weed out a prospective participant who is extremely shy or not sufficiently articulate (or intelligent) to be an effective member of the group. Essentially, an articulation question is intended to be something that will make the prospective focus group participant think a little before answering and to determine if the person is capable of providing a reasonably clear answer. Some examples of articulation questions that have proven effective are:

- If you had to move to a new community, how would you determine where to go, and what would be your biggest concerns about this move?
- What do you think the federal government should do to reduce the drug problem in our schools?
- If you won a million dollars in a lottery, would you take the money in one lump sum or in yearly installments, and why would you choose the approach you favor?
- If you could make one change that would help improve the quality of education in our schools, what would you suggest?

Each of the above questions is open ended and does not have a "right" answer. The key is that each requires the candidate to think and then provide a brief answer that demonstrates an acceptable ability to respond. Naturally, the people doing the recruiting must be provided with some parameters as to what represents an acceptable answer for this approach to be workable.

Training the Focus Group Facility Personnel to Recognize Poor Candidates for Participation

One of the most important ways to avoid problems with inarticulate or excessively shy participants is to provide direction to the people at the facility who greet the participants when they arrive and sign them in for participation. If the receptionists are told to be observant of people who are extremely shy, who are unable to communicate effectively, or who have some other strange characteristics that might inhibit their effective performance in the group, problem individuals can be eliminated before they ever are included in the group.

Communicating to the Participants That It Is Important That All of Them Share Their Views During the Group

It is often a good idea to tell the group at the beginning of a session that you (the moderator) are charged with facilitating the discussion in the room and that it is therefore essential that everyone participate in the discussion. Although this statement probably is not sufficient motivation to stimulate the less talkative people to participate actively in the discussion, it does give the moderator a tool to use for encouraging discussion. For example, if one member is not participating, it is appropriate for the moderator to direct a question or probe at this individual, first reminding the person that the moderator is expected to get information from everyone in the room. This reinforces the initial guideline that was identified and represents a directive to the less talkative person so that he or she will feel a greater obligation to participate.

Insisting on Homogeneity in the Group

One of the factors that can inhibit group discussion is a feeling of intimidation or lack of comfort among some participants based on their perceptions of others in the room. This can occur if a focus group has been configured so that some participants are perceived to be much smarter, more knowledgeable, or more influential than the others, simply on the basis of their title or company represented. Similarly, if there is a major difference in age, income, or education among the people in a group, some people can become intimidated and be less likely to be active participants in the discussion. In addition to taking care in the recruiting specifications to find people who are relatively homogeneous in their background, it is also often a good idea not to ask people for titles when they are introduced in a group situation. This is because if one person is the president of a company, another is the executive vice president for finance, and all the others are treasurers or comptrollers, the latter individuals might feel subservient to the two senior officers and therefore not be willing to go out on a limb to share their views about the topics that are discussed.

HANDLING THE DOMINANT PERSON IN A GROUP

One aspect of group dynamics that some moderators have great difficulty handling properly is the overly enthusiastic or aggressive participant who seeks to dominate the conversation. It is quite common in a focus group situation to have one individual who tries to monopolize and/or control the conversation, either by trying to answer every question asked to the participants or by lecturing to the group when providing the answer. This latter situation is often seen in medical groups when an elderly physician is placed in a group with several younger and less experienced individuals. The older doctor will often feel a need to address his or her colleagues while answering the question, but this is frequently done in the form of a short lecture as opposed to simply sharing an opinion. The net effect of this type of behavior can be to inhibit the other physicians from actively participating in the discussion for fear of looking dumb in front of this "mentor." Although this is a medical example, we have seen the same type of dynamic occurring in other types of groups from different market segments. The important point is that the moderator needs to recognize quickly the situation that is occurring and then take action to minimize its effect on the others in the room.

Using "Write-Down" Exercises

I feel that write-down exercises, which force all the participants to get involved in the discussion, are one of the most important tools for a moderator, both to stimulate discussion among the participants and also to minimize (or perhaps eliminate) negative group dynamics. A write-down exercise is essentially a moderator's request that participants in the room write down their views about an issue on paper that is provided. The amount of writing that is involved can be as little as a few words or as much as a short paragraph, but it is a vital part of the process to involve all members of the group in the discussion. Further, it has been demonstrated for many years that if people are asked a question in a group environment, they will almost certainly say what is popular in the room (or what they feel is expected of them) if they have not provided themselves with a written perspective before answering the question. If, on the other hand, they have written down their answer, they almost always will read from their sheet, even if their response is quite different from that of others in the room. This is one of the key values of write-down exercises: They will almost always get to the true feelings of the individual.

The other reason that write-down exercises are valuable is that they help less outgoing participants to take part in the discussion, given that it may be easier for these participants to share their views with this "crutch" in front of them. Also, because each of the group members has a written point of view, it is very easy for the moderator to quickly go around the room to ask each of the people to briefly state his or her view. As the views are shared, the moderator can use the other techniques discussed previously to stimulate the interaction between the participants about the views.

Using Body Language

Another technique that can be helpful in minimizing the effect of a dominant person on the group is for the moderator to use body language to communicate that he or she would like this individual to back off. Some examples of tactics that might be considered are:

- Staring at the person when he or she tries to interrupt others who are talking.
- Holding up one's hand when the dominant person starts to talk to indicate that the other person must finish before the dominant person can share his or her thoughts.
- Looking right at the person and giving him or her the *shh* gesture (placing one finger in front of the mouth) to indicate that the person does not have the right to talk at the present time.

Direct Intervention

Sometimes people do not respond to body language, or the moderator is not skilled in sending a nonverbal message to a participant. In these cases, it is necessary to use a more direct approach to ensure that the correct message is delivered. Some examples of the types of things a moderator can say in this type of situation are:

- "Bob, we need to get inputs from everyone on this subject, and we will hear from you after some of the other people have expressed their views."
- "Bob, I can tell that you are very passionate about this issue, but we really need to hear how the others feel about it."

If this person continues to be a problem, then the moderator will have to take an even more direct approach to controlling this person. One very effective technique is to intentionally ignore this individual when asking for opinions in the room. For example, if the moderator addresses a question to the group, he or she can direct special attention to calling on other participants before including the dominant person in the discussion. Normally, the dominant person will get the hint very quickly and begin to function as an equal part of the group.

If this does not work, the next step is to speak directly to this person, saying something like "Bob, you must let the other people in the group give their opinions—then we can hear from you" or "Bob, part of my responsibility is to hear from everyone in the room. You are making this very difficult, so it would be helpful if you would give the others time to share their thoughts before you give yours."

What to Do If the Situation Becomes Intolerable

Once in a great while, a participant becomes so uncooperative that there is no option but to remove him or her from the group. This is a rare phenomenon, but it does occur once every year or two, and when it happens, the moderator must understand how to accomplish this task without compromising the mission of the group. One thing that the moderator does not want to do is create a conflict situation that places the outspoken person in the role of the "bad guy" who has been thrown out of the room for lack of cooperation. If this occurs, the moderator will find that the participants left in the room will side with the person who has been asked to leave: That individual will become the victim, and most people will feel sorry for what he or she has experienced, largely because they are projecting how they would feel if they were in his or her place.

As a result, the challenge to the moderator is how to eliminate this uncooperative person from the room in such a way that it does not create negative feelings among the participants. The way I have accomplished this over the years is as follows:

- First, the experienced moderator will recognize that there is a person in the group who represents a potential problem in cooperating with the others.
- At the first opportunity, the moderator should leave the room to talk to the observers in the back room and indicate to them that there is a real concern about this individual and that it may be necessary to remove the person from the room. This is important to do to avoid confusion among the people in the back.
- The moderator should then agree with one person in the back room that if the uncooperative individual cannot be controlled, a signal will be given (e.g., a two-arm stretch, scratching the back of one's neck) to have the back room contact communicate with the facility host, who will have been told what to do by the moderator when he or she left the room.
- When the signal is given, the host will enter the focus group room and ask for the specific person, saying that this person has a phone call that requires his or her immediate attention. When the person gets outside the room, the hostess in the facility will indicate that this person is to be paid and then sent home. If the individual has left some personal item in the focus group room that is needed, the facility personnel should retrieve it, as we would not want this person to return to the room for fear of alienating the others.

This process, which is used very infrequently, does work very effectively to eliminate the uncooperative party without alienating the rest of the group. Importantly, because it is executed by a sign from the moderator to the back room, the other participants normally will not feel that the moderator caused the uncooperative party's expulsion; rather, they will feel that the phone call is legitimate. If some of the group participants ask why this person did not return to the room after the phone call, the moderator can say something like "This person was not enabling all the people in the room to have sufficient opportunities to share their thoughts, so he/she was asked not to return." This sends a message to the other participants that the moderator is very interested in their views and felt a need to eliminate one person from the room so that each of the other participants would have a chance to join in the discussion. The net effect of this scenario is that the disruptive party is eliminated from the group without diminishing the willingness of the others to continue to participate in the discussion.

UNDERSTANDING THE USE OF NONVERBAL RESPONSES

One of the biggest opportunities for a moderator to stimulate discussion in a focus group does not have anything to do with talking. Often a moderator can get as much out of what a participant says with his or her body as can be obtained from the words that are spoken about a particular topic. An experienced moderator will learn to read the nonverbal responses/body language of the people in focus groups to gauge their reactions to the topics being discussed. Most moderators agree that they can feel a sense of enthusiasm (or lack of interest) among the participants during a focus group that is independent of the nature of the conversations that occur.

Observing Nonverbal Signals

There are a few general signals that I have found to be very helpful in providing a clue that a participant (or group of people) is saying something without actually speaking the words. A trained moderator will be alert to these types of signals and will use them to draw out the people in the room on how they really feel about the topic being discussed. Some of the more obvious nonverbal signs that a moderator might encounter are

- *Signs of inattention/boredom* such as frequent yawning, leaning way back in one's chair, regularly looking at one's watch, or doodling on a pad of paper. All of these suggest that the person is not interested in the topic being discussed, and it is incumbent on the moderator to find out why.
- *Signs of defensiveness or disagreement,* which would include sitting with one's arms folded on one's chest, regularly looking up at the ceiling, and making facial expressions that would suggest disagreement with what is being discussed.

- *Signs of enthusiasm* or agreement with what is being discussed, including sitting on the front part of the chair with the body bent toward the table, as if trying to get into the center of the action. Other signs of enthusiasm toward the topic being discussed would be a sense of participants' hyperalertness to the discussions, in terms of paying close attention so that they do not lose any of the content. Also, an experienced moderator can tell by the enthusiasm with which people try to participate in the group that the topic is of interest to them. This does not necessarily mean that they feel particularly positive about the topic, but it does suggest that the topic has hit a nerve and is something that they are interested in discussing.

Using Nonverbal Signals

Once a moderator has identified a reaction from a participant or the entire group, this should be acted on as soon as possible. For example, if there is a discussion about a new service and the moderator notices one of the participants showing very negative body language, it is a good time to address this individual and say something like "Shelly, I have a sense that you might have a different view than others are expressing. Perhaps you might want to share your feelings with the group."

Another situation in which reading nonverbal signs requires some immediate action is one in which the group seems to be running out of energy and losing interest in the topic being discussed. This can be due to a number of things, such as a bad idea, a poor presentation of a good idea, time of day (i.e., late group), or the weather conditions in the area or temperature in the room. When the moderator senses this type of problem, it is often an opportune time to change the pace of the discussion by introducing a quick projective exercise (examples are discussed in Chapter 13) to energize the group. Some moderators will also take a few minutes to inject some humor in the room or will stop the discussion and pass out sweets to the participants to give them energy. It is also helpful for the moderator to get up and walk around the room, as the change in the position of the moderator will force the participants to move around in their seats, thus helping to revitalize them. In Europe, where group discussions often run longer than 2 hours, it is common for moderators to call a 15-minute recess when this type of situation occurs, but I have not found this to be viable in the United States because of the limited time available to cover the material and because of the difficulty in getting the participants focused back on the topic when the break is completed. Also, a break gives the participants an opportunity to talk to each other about the material being discussed, and this can pollute the environment relative to future topics that will be discussed.

Moderator Nonverbals

Just as the participants can provide nonverbal signs that can be interpreted by the moderator as indicative of feelings about the topics being discussed, the moderator can also provide these types of signals to the participants. The difference is that the moderator must be very careful *not* to provide any type of body language or other nonverbal signs in a focus group that might indicate to the participants that the facilitator has a bias or stake in the outcome of the sessions.

On the other hand, as indicated earlier in this chapter, an experienced moderator can use nonverbal responses very effectively to communicate to individuals in a group who are not cooperating. These are the only types of nonverbal reactions that a moderator should provide during a focus group discussion.

INVOLVING CLIENT PARTICIPANTS IN THE
FOCUS GROUP PROCESS WHILE THE GROUP IS IN SESSION

One of the major benefits of the focus group methodology is that it can involve client personnel as active participants. Unlike quantitative research, in which the client generally cannot be directly involved in the actual research as it happens (other than by occasionally monitoring a phone line), focus groups provide the opportunity for the moderator and the people in the back room behind the one-way mirror to influence the nature of the discussion in the group room.

The involvement of the people from behind the observation mirror in the group has several very important benefits. Specifically:

- It enables them to feel a sense of ownership in the group, as they can be involved in directing the discussion that occurs in the group room.

- It will often result in richer, more helpful focus groups, for the moderator cannot have the same perspective on the topics being discussed as the clients do, so additional information can be provided to the moderator during the group that will help the course of the questioning.

- It avoids "Monday morning quarterbacking" among the observers, who otherwise might complain at the end of a group that the discussion did not cover several important points—even though these may not have been included in the discussion guide.

- Finally, the interaction of the moderator and the clients in the back room can be helpful to the moderator if a subject area is raised in the group that is considered to be important, yet the moderator was not briefed on the topic before the group, and the nature of the material is such that some input to the facilitator is needed for the topic to be effectively covered. With the focus group setup, the moderator has a chance to get this information from the client personnel and then incorporate it into the group discussion to maximize the value of the inputs obtained.

This section will review how this interaction has traditionally occurred and will describe a relatively new approach at facilitating moderator-client interchange during the group.

The Traditional Approach to
Moderator-Client Interaction

The most common way clients communicate to their moderator during a focus group is to pass a note into the room by asking one of the hosts at the facility to present it to the moderator. This might occur once during a focus group session or as often as 10 times, depending on the nature of the subject matter, the quality of the moderator, and the personal needs of the clients in the back room.

In addition to passing notes into the room, some clients still require the moderator to wear a "wire" so that they can talk directly to the moderator via the earpiece while the group is in progress.

Why the Traditional Approach
Should Not Be Used

There are several key reasons why the traditional approach (sending notes into the room) should not be used if the client is really interested in maximizing the quality of the output from focus group research:

- *It slows the momentum in the focus group room and takes participants' minds off the topic being covered, thus making it more difficult to resume the discussion.* This occurs because the process of sending a note into the room requires that the door be opened, which will immediately stop the conversation while the participants look to see who (and why) someone has entered the room. Then the moderator must take the time to read the note; this precludes direction of the group discussion and further increases the distraction.

- *It often will prove to be an unclear communication for the moderator, who then has to figure out what to do with the request in order to satisfy the people in the back room.* For example, often the notes are written very quickly with an emphasis on brevity, and both of these factors complicate the moderator's ability to read and interpret the note. Then the moderator will have to figure out how to incorporate this information into the group discussion so as to generate the best inputs from the participants. In some cases, the moderator may have a specific reason for not addressing the suggested area at that time but does not have the forum to explain this to the client.

- *Sending notes into the group room encourages sloppy observation techniques by the people behind the one-way mirror.* Because back room participants are permitted to send notes into the room when issues arise that they feel are important, it is not uncommon for them to feel a need to constantly be sending in directions to the moderator. However, if a moderator is experienced in the profession and has had an effective briefing, there is an excellent chance that the topic that he or she was asked to cover in the note will be discussed later in the group. Further, letting people send notes into the room encourages back room participants to spend more time thinking about what they want to say to the moderator than focusing on the inputs obtained from the discussion. In effect, the notes become a "knee-jerk" reaction based more on impulse than on a real need for the information.

- *The process of sending notes into the room also serves to undermine the role of the moderator in the focus group process.* As indicated in an earlier chapter, a key reason the focus group methodology works is that the moderator is the authority figure in the room who directs the discussion. If notes are coming into the room with instructions to the moderator, this changes the nature of the discussion, and the participants will begin to feel that the real authority is in the back room. This will result in participants' focusing on directing their answers to the back room observers rather than the moderator, which will result in loss of control over the group and a significant reduction in the overall quality of the information generated.

The Modern Approach to Moderator/Client Interaction

A more effective way to conduct moderator-client interaction during the focus group is to have face-to-face communication between the two parties. This can happen if the moderator is trained in organizing the discussion guide so that there are times during the group when it is possible to leave the focus group room and go behind the mirror to talk with the observers. This becomes a very beneficial process because the moderator can now talk directly with observers who have questions or comments about what is happening in the room, and there is no impact on the authority role of the moderator or question as to what the person desired the moderator to do, as might occur with a handwritten note. Normally, it is very easy for a moderator to arrange to come to the back room two to four times during the focus group, and this should be more than acceptable for the client because it means that the client will have effective communication. This helps ensure that the group discussion will achieve the goals that have been established.

To go to the back room without having this affect the overall quality of the group, the moderator needs to understand and implement a few key elements. First, at the beginning of the group (during the introduction), it is useful to tell the participants that you will be leaving the room a few times during the groups in order to check your detailed notes in the back. Another approach is to tell the participants that you have a colleague who keeps track of everything that is said in the group in order to enable the content to be consistent with the other sessions, and it is necessary for you to go into the back to check the charts to ensure that you have not forgotten to cover all the essential points. Although some people do it, I am not a believer in telling the participants that you are going to the back room to talk to the client personnel, as this can affect the authority role of the moderator, as alluded to previously.

Another important parameter is that the participants in the room must be given a written exercise to accomplish while the moderator is out of the room, along with instructions that they are not to talk with each other when the moderator is not present. This is to keep them from talking about the topics being discussed without the moderator around so that they do not pollute the environment for future discussion or cover important points that the moderator should hear.

It is also important for the moderator to ensure that the people in the back room understand that only a very limited amount of time can be spent talking while the group members are doing their exercise. Generally, a moderator should not spend more than 1 to 2 minutes in the back room talking to the observers. This means that the people in the back must understand that they should raise only essential topics with the moderator and that they should explain their concerns clearly and succinctly so that the moderator can assimilate the information and incorporate it into the discussion that will follow upon returning to the room.

In summary, the fundamental elements of conducting successful focus groups can be characterized as sharing a "velvet glove" approach. The moderator must use all tools, including an approachable demeanor, to get all relevant, open, and honest information and reactions from the group without leading their responses or inhibiting them in any way. At the same time, the moderator will use verbal and visual techniques to maintain total control over the group dynamics and the information flow of the groups. This means that a variety of activities and stimuli should always be available to the moderator in anticipation of unforeseen issues or obstacles that may arise.

13

ADVANCED MODERATING TECHNIQUES

This chapter will focus on a series of techniques that moderators can use during focus groups to improve the overall quality of the information generated. The techniques can be divided into the following three basic categories:

- *Techniques to "manage" group dynamics*—These techniques are aimed at helping a moderator minimize some of the problems that are frequently associated with group dynamics, such as participants who are intimidated by having to talk in front of the others or the need of some people to conform to the views of the others in the room even if they feel differently about the topic being discussed.

- *Techniques to "energize" a tired group*—Sometimes a moderator will sense that the participants in the room are getting tired and therefore are not being as spontaneous or forthright with their comments as might be desired. This can be a function of the time of day (i.e., late), the climatic conditions (hot!), or the day of the week when the sessions are conducted (people tend to be more tired later in the work week than on Monday or Tuesday).

- *Techniques to "peel the onion" a little more than normal*—These are tools aimed at helping a moderator delve further into the minds of the participants than might normally occur with traditional questioning. They are exercises aimed at stretching the participants' minds by providing different ways for them to think about and articulate their feelings regarding a particular topic.

It is very important that moderators become familiar with all of these techniques and with others that they might create for themselves. This is because it is not unusual for a moderator to have to reach into his or her "bag of tricks" while a group is in session to introduce a new exercise when the discussion is not providing the information that will achieve the objectives of the research. Though it is always best to plan the use of activities such as those discussed in this chapter, often the need for them will come up spontaneously during a group, and the moderator has to be sufficiently comfortable with the techniques to introduce them on the fly.

The many different techniques described in the pages that follow are not appropriate for all types of groups or for all target audiences. The effective moderator will use only the techniques that are needed to address a specific situation as part of achieving the research objectives. Although there may be several ways to accomplish a goal, it is important that only one be used in a group to ensure that the participants remain interested and engaged.

TECHNIQUES TO HELP MANAGE GROUP DYNAMICS

The following summarizes the two general types of activities that a moderator can use to increase the likelihood that all group participants will be willing to share their views about a particular topic and will not be influenced by what others have said before them. Each of these techniques has been field tested over a period of years and has proven successful when implemented properly by the moderator. The techniques are based on the following two theoretical premises, which are derived from academic and business learning:

- In a group environment, participants who have written down what they plan to say are more likely to state their opinion about a topic than those who are asked the question without having previously committed their thoughts to writing.
- Individuals are more comfortable talking in a group environment when they can refer to some type of written stimuli before being required to speak.

Below are summarized the two types of exercises that are employed to minimize the negative effects of group dynamics while stimulating people to participate in the discussion.

Write-Down Exercises

This group of moderating tools normally involves the preparation of forms that the participants complete at specific times during the session to formalize their views on a topic. I find it helpful to use one or two write-down exercises relevant to the topic to be discussed at the start of the group so that they can be used to facilitate the warm-up discussion. Often the first 15 to 20 minutes of a group consists of a group discussion about the information that was generated in the initial write-down exercises.

The following will review several types of write-down exercises that we use regularly. In each case, the objective is to give participants an opportunity to think about the response they will want to give in the group discussion and to provide them with the "crutch" of their own words on the topic in order to encourage them to give their true opinion once the discussion has begun.

First Thoughts and Overall Ratings

This is a frequently used exercise aimed at obtaining top-of-mind reactions to a specific array of products or services. A sample form is shown in Table 13.1. The exercise accomplishes several different tasks for the moderator:

1. It gives the moderator a sense of the group's level of awareness of and familiarity with the items included in the exercise.

Table 13.1   First Thoughts and Overall Ratings

Description	Overall Reaction (10-Point Scale)	First Thoughts

2. It communicates an overall attitude toward the item/category that can be used by the moderator to stimulate discussion among the participants. For example, if a 10-point scale is used to rate the specific product, the moderator's first action might be to identify the people on the extremes and use that information to stimulate discussion among them to determine the reasons for their feelings.

3. It provides a few words or sentences that describe why the person feels the way he or she does. This can be helpful to individuals when they give their views to the group and can be useful to the moderator as reminder material when he or she is writing the final report of the sessions.

Importance of Characteristics

Another exercise that can be very effective in a focus group environment uses a list of characteristics that relate to a particular product, serv-

Table 13.2 Importance of Characteristics

Characteristic	Overall Rating (10-Point Scale)	Comments

ice, or decision to help the moderator gauge the importance of each of the characteristics. In addition to rating the importance, participants also indicate briefly why they have rated the individual items as they have. An example of this exercise is shown in Table 13.2.

This type of exercise is very helpful in a group discussion for the following reasons:

- It provides the moderator with perspective on which of the characteristics are most important to the various people in the room. I usually ask the participants to indicate the three most (and sometimes the three least) important characteristics on their list. Then I survey the group to see where the preferences fall. This input is used to begin the in-depth questioning of the participants about their reasons for selecting the item as important or not important. With all the information right in front of the participants, they generally share their true personal preferences regardless of the responses of others.

- This approach is also helpful in determining if any characteristics are missing that should have been considered. Because the participants have a list of many different items, they may be stimulated to identify other factors that are important but have been omitted from the list. If the group discussion indicates that additional characteristics are important to the group overall, it may be worthwhile to incorporate them into subsequent group exercises in the same research series.

Preference Ratings

One of the most common uses of write-down exercises is managing the discussion of preferences among participants about a particular topic being discussed. For example, if a new product concept is presented to a focus group, an excellent way to determine how people feel about it is to use a preference chart. This type of exercise would normally include at least the following specific elements:

- An attitude or preference rating, normally stated using a numerical scale. I always use a 10-point "smiley" scale as I find people very comfortable with this format. It is very important that the participants understand that they are being asked for the rating that represents their own view about the topic and not that of the marketplace. When a moderator is not clear about this point, participants often give a positive rating but later explain that even though they do not like the idea for themselves, they felt it was a good idea and would appeal to many other people.
- An explanation of the perceived strengths and limitations of the idea. This should be provided in as much detail as possible because it will be useful to the participants as they are asked to share their views with the others in the room. It also can become a valuable resource for the moderator, who might use it to refresh his or her memory when preparing the notes to write the report.
- Sometimes other elements such as the anticipated price of the product or service, the expected customer group to which participants feel it would appeal, or even the likelihood that they would purchase the item in the near future. All of these (and many other ideas) can be useful write-down inputs if they do not become too burdensome for participants to complete.

Position-Fixing Exercises

These are a slightly different type of exercise from the traditional "write-down" in that they normally are not preplanned and generally are much less comprehensive. Position-fixing exercises are intended to lock participants into a particular point of view about a topic that arises during the discussion so that the moderator can leverage the differences in the group to stimulate further discussion. Normally, when using this exercise, the moderator asks the participants to write down no more than a word or a sentence to reflect a particular point of view about a topic being discussed. Some examples of how position fixing might be used are

- Asking participants in a group to indicate the amount of time they spend reading books for pleasure each week. This is the type of question that some people might not answer honestly if it were not a write-down, as the peer pressure from the rest of the group could affect their answer. For example, if the people who answered before them all said they read for several hours per week, participants might have trouble saying that they read 20 minutes or less. However, once they have written their answer down, people will normally provide the truth.
- Asking the participants to identify the brand of whiskey they drink (assuming that the group was recruited for this specification). Without knowledge of what others are going to say, people generally indicate what they really do consume regularly. However, if they do not write down this information, many people are inclined to indicate that they consume only the best or most prestigious brands.
- Seeking a quick, spontaneous reaction to a new idea in the group by asking people to indicate their attitudes using the 10-point scale. The participants are simply asked to put the number that corresponds to their feeling in a circle they make on their pad, and the moderator collects this information by going around the room and asking each person for his or her ratings. The key is to determine who is for the idea and who is against it so that the moderator can use this information to stimulate the group discussion among the people in the room.

TECHNIQUES TO ENERGIZE A GROUP

The following techniques generally have a dual purpose in focus groups. The first is to recharge the people in the group so they can become revitalized and be more effective participants. The second is to gain some additional insights from the participants that add depth to the overall discussion of the topic. These exercises change the intellectual focus of the group by adding an exercise that is viewed by the group as unusual and perhaps even fun. As a result, there is generally a renewed level of energy among the participants, which then stimulates more active discussion.

Like position-fixing exercises, these techniques are almost never planned in advance. Because their primary purpose is to revitalize a group that appears to have become tired or bored, a moderator will never know when it may be necessary to use the specific techniques. The following will summarize the exercises that I have found to be most effective in achieving this goal.

Nonsense Associations

In this exercise, the participants are asked to indicate an item from one predetermined grouping that they most closely associate with the product, service, or institution being discussed in the group. It is essential that the item being discussed in the group have no direct or indirect relationship to the category selected for the nonsense association. For example, in a focus group that is evaluating a new hand-held computer, it is 9:00 in the evening, the group is getting tired, and the moderator decides to take a small diversionary trip to re-energize the group. At this point, the moderator might ask all the participants to write down the automobile they associate most closely with this hand-held computer and also to write a few sentences that describe why they selected that car.

Participants may view this type of exercise as silly, stupid, or perhaps just a waste of time. However, evoking those emotions will help to achieve the basic goal of the exercise, which is to energize them so they can be productive for the rest of the session. When this type of resistance arises, the moderator can ask the participant to "grin and bear it" and humor the moderator by participating in the exercise.

In the car example, people might compare the product to, for example, a Mercedes (implying high quality, good engineering, and high price), a Chevrolet (suggesting average quality and lower price), or a Toyota (suggesting economy, good quality, and not particularly high price). The brief discussion in the group about the cars that people select and the rationale for this will serve as comic relief for the group and also will give the moderator some insights into how the people in the room feel about the product or service.

Three other nonsense associations that I have used successfully are

1. *Animals*—By selecting the animal that most closely is associated with a particular product, people expose real differences in product perception. People who select bears or pussycats clearly see the product differently from others who choose bats, snakes, or cheetahs.
2. *Foods*—This is also a very helpful category, as the connotation of a hamburger versus a steak or an egg versus a coconut would reveal distinctly different feelings that the participants have about the product or service being discussed.
3. *Colors*—Using colors for a nonsense association can be very effective as long as the product or service being evaluated does not already have a color associated with it. For example, if the groups were about McDonald's, we would have a built-in bias for yellow and red, and if it were for IBM, the bias would be toward blue. In these situations, using colors for this exercise probably would have no value. However, when colors are not directly associated with a product or service, it is easy to see how the reactions of a white, yellow, or pink might connote different feelings than green, brown, or purple.

Anthropomorphization

This is another focus group technique that can provide both "energy pills" for the group and useful insights into the feelings of the participants about the topic being discussed. Assuming, for example, that the item being discussed is a new type of toothpaste, the group would be asked to tell a story about the toothpaste, making the toothpaste into a real person. The direction to the group would be to give the toothpaste a name and a gender, tell its age, and provide a short paragraph that describes what type of person this toothpaste is in terms of marital and family status, interests, personality traits, and other relevant information.

The exercise is sufficiently bizarre so that most people in the room will find it fun to do, with the result that their energy level will be raised, in keeping with the objectives that have been established for this impromptu situation. The discussion that follows will normally provide some very useful information, such as

- Which gender the product is more likely to appeal to
- Which age group it is more likely to appeal to
- Whether it would be for outgoing people or for those on the fringe and, indirectly, whether it is likable
- The overall user-friendliness of the product

In essence, this exercise will get into the brand character in a way that is very difficult to accomplish with any other activities. As the participants provide details on the characters they have created, they add depth and texture to the overall insights into the product being discussed.

TECHNIQUES TO HELP "PEEL BACK THE ONION"

There are many different focus group moderating techniques available to assist a moderator in delving just a little further into the reasons why people feel the way they have indicated in a group discussion. Like the other techniques discussed in this section, the following exercises are not appropriate for all types of focus group situations or even for every demographic group included in the sessions. However, when effectively employed, they can help stimulate the thinking of the participants and help them articulate feelings that may lie below the surface. The following will summarize the principal techniques that I have found to be successful in recent years to accomplish this goal.

Personality Association

This is a technique whereby participants in a focus group are asked to use pictures (normally cut out of magazines) that are provided in the group to indicate their associations with a particular product or service. There are two broad categories of *personality association*, with the following providing a description of each.

Fixed Personality Association

In this approach, the moderator uses a standard group of pictures (generally less than 30) to help participants articulate their views about a particular product or service. An example of a fixed personality board we have used for many years is shown in Figure 13.1.

This tool has been used scores of times to gain insight into the imagery of a product, service, or institution through the people who use the item. The focus of the exercise is to get the people in the groups to identify which of the people in the chart definitely do and which definitely do not purchase or use the specific item in question. The moderator shows the board to the group, gives them a very brief time to write down their feelings, and then tallies the results on an easel. The tallies then become the basis for the discussion, with the focus on understanding why some participants feel that certain people on the board would be likely to use the service and why they feel that others would be unlikely to use it.

A major benefit of the fixed personality association is that the resource material does not have to be collected specifically for each group (as with variable personality association). Thus, the approach is convenient for the moderator to use. Another major advantage occurs the more the moderator uses the technique and becomes familiar with the characterizations of the various people on the board. This familiarity enables the moderator to recognize when a participant's judgment does not conform to the norm and then to probe the rationale behind this judgment. The disadvantage of this technique is that it does not work for all situations because it is not flexible in changing the personalities and may not focus on a sufficiently narrow group of personality choices.

Figure 13.1. The People Board

Variable Personality Association

This technique operates very similarly to the fixed association technique, except that the number of pictures used is not predefined and the selection of the situations chosen is different for every project. Some moderators prefer this approach because it is possible to tailor it more to the specific needs of the situation. Others have problems with it because it is often very difficult to find enough relevant pictures to generate the type of inputs that will be helpful to the process. Some people also feel that the time required to collect appropriate pictures is not worthwhile in terms of the payoff at the conclusion of the process.

Conceptual Mapping

This is a helpful technique that can provide a significant amount of information about how the target consumer views the product or service category being discussed and how it might relate to other similar items. It is effective only for established products because the consumer needs to have a frame of reference about both the product (or service) being evaluated and the competitive set.

The implementation of this technique starts with the moderator asking the participants to draw a tic-tac-toe type diagram (or providing them with one previously drawn on a page) that contains nine boxes, as shown below.

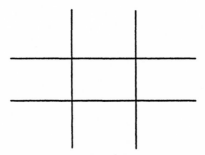

Let us assume that the focus groups are about business magazines, with the client being *Forbes*. In this situation, the participants are asked to include in the boxes shown all the different business magazines of which they are aware, with the directive that they should put magazines that are essentially the same in the same box. They can have as many (or few) magazines as they want in each box and can use as many boxes as they want to designate the groupings. Thus, if the nine boxes are not enough, they can draw another line and provide three more.

After the participants have done the exercise, the moderator starts questioning the group, with a focus on at least the following areas:

- *The awareness of the various magazines.* Although this is not quantitative research, one certainly can learn something about top-of-mind awareness by seeing which magazines were included in the charts.
- *The category visualization in the minds of the consumers.* Why did they develop the groupings that have been created in the various boxes? What did the group mean to them? This would elicit terms and distinctions such as *quality magazines,* magazines for big business versus small business, and international versus domestic publications.
- Probably most important, the placement of the magazines in the boxes. For example, if some people put *Forbes* in the same box with *Fortune,* others put it with *Business Week,* and a few put it alone, this arrangement gives the moderator an excellent tool to understand what was in the consumers' minds when they made the comparison. For example, is *Forbes* really like *Fortune*? If so, in what way? Why should *Forbes* be placed in a box by itself (as it was classified by some people)? Does that mean it is really different from the competition?

The technique can be implemented quickly or can become the major focus of a session, depending on the amount of material the moderator needs to cover and the quality of the outputs that are being generated by this discussion.

Attitudinal Scaling

Whereas conceptual mapping provides an overall assessment of the category and of the product being evaluated, it does not provide information on specific characteristics that might be important to the client organization. One could say that it offers a one-dimensional assessment, a foundation on which to build more detail.

Because the *attitudinal scaling* technique is implemented much like conceptual mapping, it would not be appropriate to use both in the same group, as they would probably conflict with each other. The plan to use attitudinal scaling starts with the recognition that two dominant characteristics about a product or service must be evaluated in the discussion to achieve the objectives of the research. For example, let us assume that in the cellular phone category, the characteristics of quality of reception and price of the phone are the dominant factors that determine which brand will be selected.

To implement this technique, the participant is asked to draw a diagram like the one shown below (or is given this information on a preprinted sheet).

The participant is then asked to write down all the brands of portable telephones of which they are aware, being sure to indicate where they fall on the quality and pricing scale. (We have found that this exercise, unlike the conceptual mapping exercise, to be a useful way to learn about gaps in the marketplace and therefore can be effective in a new product situation.) After this exercise is completed, the moderator can probe deeply into at least the following areas:

- *Levels of awareness of the different brands.* If everyone in the group writes down one or two brands but only a couple of people mention a different one, this provides some indication of top-of-mind awareness. Findings will have to be confirmed in quantitative research, but these group reactions provide a preliminary reading of levels of familiarity with the category brands.

- *The relative feeling of the consumer toward the quality and service of both the client product and the competition.* This can then form the basis for an in-depth discussion with the participants about why they consider Brand X, Y ,or Z to be high or low quality and why they feel as they do about the cost of the equipment.

Conjoint

Conjoint is generally called trade-off analysis and is a quantitative research technique. It was a popular quantitative method in the 1980s to help companies design hard goods products when they had to make major decisions regarding such things as weight, size, horsepower, and capacity. The implementation of a conjoint study is complex and requires sophisticated statistics. However, we have adapted this technique for use in the focus group environment as follows.

1. The moderator works with the client organization to determine the three to five variables that are most likely to affect the consumer's decision regarding the item to be covered in the groups.
2. Once the variables are covered, the moderator develops a write-down exercise that asks the participants to make choices among the various selections. For example, would they prefer a 13-inch screen and 4-gig hard drive or a 15-inch screen and a 3-gig hard drive? A 4-gig hard drive at a $2,700 price or a 3-gig hard drive at a $2,300 price? The consumer might be asked to make 10 to 20 of these judgments.
3. The discussion begins. The moderator might start by asking which were the easiest and the hardest decisions to make and might probe the participants about why they feel this way.
4. The moderator delves into the details of the hard decisions to determine what is really driving the consumers in terms of the features that seem to have the most influence.

Our experience is that an effective moderator can generate a significant amount of very useful information from this type of discussion and that normally the outputs are much richer and more insightful than one would obtain without using this tool to force trade-offs.

SUMMARY

In summary, exercises conducted during focus groups can be enormously helpful to the moderator in generating the maximum quality of information from the research effort. Many people do not use exercises in groups because they have difficulty implementing them in a way that generates useful outputs. The examples that were identified in this chapter are all relatively easy to execute and are proven winners in terms of being able to provide that extra edge to the moderator. I suggest that you try a few of them and then develop some of your own to share with other moderators in the industry.

14

UNIQUE MODERATING SITUATIONS

One of the greatest pleasures of working in the focus group industry is the wide variety of different types of assignment in which you can become involved. This provides an ongoing stream of intellectual challenges for the moderator, who is required to assimilate information about a large number of unrelated topics while working with very different target segments.

During the early days of focus groups, in the late 1950s and 1960s, the majority of sessions were commissioned by traditional consumer goods manufacturers. At that time, most of the groups were conducted among women head of household and dealt with packaged goods or health and beauty aids products. As the technique became more popular, the uses of focus groups expanded to different types of products and services, which meant that more varied type of consumers had to be included in the research. This necessitated applying some different methods in order to maximize the effectiveness of the research among each of the target constituencies.

The purpose of this chapter is to address some of the more common *atypical* focus group types in order to provide the benefit of my personal experience conducting sessions with these types of people. Although some of the suggestions may not represent major changes in the approach to conducting the groups with the segments, I have found them to be important in terms of getting the maximum out of the research with each of the different target audiences.

PHYSICIAN FOCUS GROUPS

Focus groups with the medical profession represent some of the most interesting and challenging work I have done in my career. However, to maximize the effectiveness of focus groups with this market segment, it is very important for a moderator to seriously consider each of the following suggestions.

Recruiting

Because of last-minute emergencies, cancellations by doctors who agreed to attend focus groups are very common. Therefore, it is important to significantly over-recruit for the groups to ensure that enough physicians are in attendance to have a viable discussion. For example, if the goal is to have 9 to 10 doctors in the group, it would be wise to recruit 13 or 14, recognizing that occasionally it will be necessary to pay some of them their honoraria and send them home because too many show up. This is far preferred to having a session with only 5 or 6 doctors in attendance because of last-minute cancellations.

In addition, it is imperative that the physicians be told to come to the focus group facility at least 15 minutes before the groups are scheduled to begin if the groups are to start on time. Doctors are notoriously late, and if they are told the session will start at 6:00, many of the participants will not show up until 6:10 or later.

Another issue that emerges with medical focus groups is one of past participation. Whereas it is traditional in consumer groups to screen out people who have participated in a focus group in the past 3 to 6 months, this is not a viable option for medical participant recruiting. Because of the limited number of physicians—particularly specialists—in any area, and because of the heavy demand for pharmaceutical research, it is virtually impossible to find sufficient doctors to participate who have not recently been part of a focus group.

Administrative Details

There are a few important executional details relative to the implementation of groups with physicians that should be incorporated into the sessions:

- The name tags used in the groups should identify the physicians by their first names. One of the mistakes that many moderators make when conducting physician focus groups is to use the official title *Dr.* on the name tags identifying the participants. By using a professional title for the participants and not for the moderator, an environment has been established that places the moderator at a psychological disadvantage to the participants, and this could (and often will) affect the moderator's ability to achieve the authority role that is so important in medical sessions.
- It is also essential to establish ground rules about phones and pagers in the room. If this is not done, the physicians will feel they have the license to come and go from the group room as desired to handle their pages. Although true emergencies should be addressed, having physicians leave the room to answer multiple phone messages is very disruptive to the process and can seriously affect the overall quality of the groups.
- Confidentiality is a uniquely important issue when considering medical focus groups. Although the content of a focus group should always be kept confidential by the participants (who should be asked to sign a paper on this before or after the group), in medical sessions confidentiality is even more significant than normal. This is because the doctors are always talking to colleagues and drug representatives, and confidential information that gets into the wrong hands can result in very unpleasant legal activities and serious loss of good will between moderators and their clients (even if the moderator has no direct role in the breach of security).

Moderation Issues

There are also a few unique issues regarding the moderating of medical groups:

- It is important that the moderator take control of the group immediately upon entering the room so that there is no question who is determining the flow of the discussion. The nature of the medical position is that doctors are normally the people in charge of the situation, and some have difficulty taking a subservient role in a group environment, particularly when they do not have an official reporting relationship to the "leader." As a result, the moderator should assert him- or herself very early in the group to demonstrate that an agenda will be followed and that its flow will be determined by the moderator and not the physicians.

- One of the most significant challenges that nonmedical moderators face in medical groups is the complexity of the subject matter and the need to know enough of the technical information to be able to lead the groups successfully. It is therefore important that the moderator recognize that conducting focus groups in the medical profession will normally require a great deal more preparation than for consumer groups, and this should be built into the pricing structure.

- Further, it is imperative that the moderator understand the value of participants' questions when conducting groups in the medical industry. For example, when discussing a new product concept, it is common for the participants to have questions about the drug or the procedure that they ask the moderator. However, if the concept statement (or other external stimulus) has been effectively prepared, these questions probably are really indicative of concerns the physicians have about various aspects of the topic being discussed. Therefore, rather than attempting to answer questions that are raised in the group, we find it much more useful to probe for the reason why the physician is asking the question. This line of follow-up questioning will often generate very important information that was probably not considered when developing the concept statement and can provide important depth to the discussion.

EMPLOYEE FOCUS GROUPS

This research is executed among employees of an organization for the purpose of obtaining inputs on employee morale, staffing changes, new benefit programs, or other initiatives that affect the workforce. A few key guidelines should be considered when implementing focus groups in an employee environment to increase the likelihood of the project's success. The most important of them are discussed below.

Recruitment

The recruiting for employee sessions should bring together people who are at approximately the same level in the organization so that the position of one individual does not intimidate or otherwise influence the others. Also, it is advantageous to recruit people from different parts of the organization so as to minimize the chances that the participants will have a personal or professional relationship with each other. In the ideal situation, none of the employees know each other, but this is very difficult to accomplish unless the sessions are being conducted in a very large company with huge numbers of employees in the same general location.

Backgrounding

In contrast to practice with other focus groups, we find it particularly helpful for the moderator to give participants in an employee session a brief statement of the purpose of the groups and the likely use of the results. This will normally help secure the full cooperation of the participants, as they will recognize the value of the contribution they are making to the organization.

Security Issues

In the context of employee focus groups, addressing individuals' concerns about security and confidentiality is extremely important. Specifically, most employees will not share their real feelings about a topic in a focus group environment unless they are assured that the output will never come back to haunt them. Therefore, during the implementation of employee groups, moderators should consider the following guidelines:

- Tell the groups that the company does not provide the last names of employees to the moderator, thereby reassuring the employees that it would be impossible to identify them in the final report or through conversation with the research contacts in the organization.
- Conduct the sessions in a company conference room that does not have a one-way mirror. Employee groups implemented in facilities with a one-way mirror will normally not work very well, as the participants may feel that they are being observed by their supervisor or other members of management of the organization, and this can inhibit their responses.
- Assure the participants that there is no tape of the proceedings (audio or video) so that it will not be possible to trace any individual comments back to a participant.
- Do whatever is necessary to reassure the participants that the moderator is independent and is not a "spy" for company management.

TEEN GROUPS

Those of us who have had teenagers know that most of them live in a world that is uniquely focused on themselves. Typical teens do not consider planning as important to their daily existence, nor do they tend to place the same priority on punctuality as would their parents. As a result, a moderator should consider a few key guidelines when planning and implementing focus groups with this segment.

Recruiting

As a general practice, it is advisable to significantly over-recruit for teen groups. If our goal is to have 10 participants in a session, we normally will recruit 16 to 18 teens because they tend to forget or just decide not to come to the groups at the last minute. Also, it is imperative that the teens understand that they will not be invited to come into the groups or get paid for coming if they are not at the facility on time, as punctuality is very difficult for many of the teens to accept as being important.

Group Composition

There are two important issues of group composition when planning sessions with teens:

1. The ages of the teens in the room cannot differ by more than 2 or 3 years (particularly in the early teens), because the ability of this age group to relate to their peers is best when there is no more than about 1 year of difference in age.
2. Teen groups should not be conducted with participants of the opposite sex. At this age, the hormones are raging, and when boys and girls are included in the same group they get distracted and self-conscious, which can seriously impede their ability to concentrate on the subject matter and to be honest and forthright with their opinions.

Technique

Generally it is more difficult to stimulate teens (particularly boys) to be active participants in focus groups. Most teenagers tend to want to answer questions with the shortest possible response and will not share more than they are asked to comment upon. Further, they tend to have a fairly short attention span and can easily become bored with the topic being discussed. As a result of this, moderators who work with teens should consider the following:

- Maintain as high an energy level as possible in the room in order to maintain the attention of the participants. If the moderator communicates high energy, this will generally be reflected in the participants.
- Provide variety in the way topics are discussed and the number of different areas covered. This is important to keeping the teens' interest level high.

- Ensure that the moderator is always aware of who is and who is not volunteering to participate in the discussion. Often a very verbal teen will try to dominate the conversation, and this will prove to be intimidating to some of the others. As a result, it is important for the moderator to continually draw the shyer participants into the discussion by asking them direct questions, rather than relying on them to volunteer participation.

Food

A vital element in teen focus groups is the availability of snacks and soft drinks in the room. This age group will respond better if they are eating while talking, and healthy snacks that enhance energy will be helpful to the overall process.

KIDS' GROUPS

There are some definite similarities in the guidelines for conducting groups with kids versus teens. However, there also are enough differences so that the topic requires a separate discussion. This section focuses on kids 7 to 10 years old, as we find that research done with children younger than this is more like play experiences viewed by people behind a mirror than a traditional focus group. The following are some of the important considerations when conducting focus groups among children in the 7- to 10-year age segment.

Recruiting

Our experience is that focus groups with kids work best when conducted with 5 to 7 children rather than the traditional 8 to 10. This is because of the less structured environment needed for groups with children, which in turn requires more attention by the moderator just to maintain a sense of order in the room.

Length

Most moderators who work with kids find that the optimal length of the session is 60 to 80 minutes. It is very difficult to do a kids' group that is more than about 80 minutes, as the children get restless and the moderator begins to lose their attention and can have problems maintaining control over the room.

Administrative Details

Children who participate in focus groups must be told in a firm but friendly manner that there are rules in the session to which they must adhere. Further, the moderator must be willing to remind the children of the rules during the groups, recognizing that the younger children have very short attention spans and tend to forget what they have been told only a few minutes earlier.

Content

Due to the shorter length of the typical kids' group, it is important that the discussion guide and overall strategic objectives for the session be very focused so that the maximum amount of time can be spent working on the topics that are of greatest import. Whereas in adult groups it is often helpful to have lengthy warm-up sessions, this is not advisable with children because the early part of the group is when the moderator normally will have the best attention of the participants.

It is helpful to use external stimuli as much as possible in kids' groups so that the children have something to react to that they can see (and possibly touch). This will increase their overall interest in the idea and help to involve all the children in the group.

Room Setup

There are mixed opinions among moderators as to the optimal arrangement for a focus group room where children are involved. However, the following should provide some guidelines:

- Ideally, there should not be a table separating the moderator from the children, so a semicircle setting of chairs is optimal.
- If the children are to be asked to write down anything during the group, appropriate desk or table space must be available, as they will have difficulty with clipboards or writing on their lap.

- The room should be light and airy but without access to anything that might distract the attention of the children. For example, the shades or blinds in the room should be drawn so that the children do not become fixated on something happening outside when they should be concentrating on what is occurring in the room.

SENSITIVE TOPICS

One of the most difficult types of groups to conduct is one in which the moderator is required to lead a discussion of a topic that can be embarrassing or emotionally draining. For example, I have conducted groups with women who have lost their husband in the past 6 months, men who have just begun recovering after a heart attack, and men and women (separate sessions) who are incontinent. To conduct these types of groups effectively requires some special personal and professional skills. For example:

- One of the most important considerations in conducting groups on very sensitive topics is for the moderator to be very serious and professional about the mission he or she has with the people. If the participants understand that you are a professional and take your work seriously, they are much more likely to participate enthusiastically.
- The moderator must recognize that these types of topics are much more difficult for the participants to discuss and that it is therefore important to show empathy and patience when facilitating the discussion. The participants may become emotional or be reluctant to speak, and the moderator cannot become annoyed with this behavior, or it will be obvious to the participants and will have the opposite effect from what was intended.
- The moderator can also help the situation significantly by making a statement at the beginning of the session that identifies the shared characteristic of the group of people in the room. For example, if all group members recognize that they have been recruited for the group because of problems with incontinence, then they will tend to feel some comfort in their numbers and will normally be more at ease talking about the issues.

- We also believe that it is often better to have a more senior moderator (in both age and experience) when dealing with very sensitive topics. Although young moderators can be successful in these types of groups, an older individual is more likely to establish a reassuring rapport and communicate the necessary empathy.

- It is advisable to avoid videotaping very sensitive groups because the camera can be intimidating and may inhibit participation. Although an experienced moderator can usually make the groups forget that a camera is present, this can be difficult when the discussion topic itself creates some discomfort. When a camera is used in these situations, the client should be warned that it can have a negative impact on the willingness of some people in the room to share their views.

VERY OLD SENIOR CITIZENS

As the population of the United States continues to age, more and more focus groups will be conducted with elderly people because they will account for a greater percentage of the population and buying power. A few important considerations must be built into a research plan when conducting groups with the elderly, whom for the purpose of this discussion we will define as 65+ years of age:

- The moderator must be particularly patient and tolerant with this age group. Older citizens do not move or think as quickly as the younger people, yet what they feel or have to say can be just as valuable to the focus group research. A moderator must be willing to explain things more precisely (and perhaps several times) to older citizens when doing focus groups.

- The pace of focus groups with older people must be somewhat slower than with a younger target market. This requires covering fewer topics and allocating more time to each.

- A moderator also must realize that some of the older citizens do not hear, see, or talk as well as younger respondents. It is important for a moderator to be tolerant of these limitations.

- Another important consideration when planning groups with older people involves the time of day when the groups can be held.

Unlike the typical groups, which tend to be at 6:00 and 8:00 in the evening, most sessions with older people should be conducted during the day. Older people have difficulty with evening sessions, not only because they are frequently too tired to perform in the evening but also because they are often very reluctant to go out after dark.

- Finally, it is often necessary to provide transportation to the facility for older citizens. We have had excellent success in concentrated metropolitan areas using vans to pick up and deliver the participants. This has the benefit of ensuring that the people arrive on time, and it also generally is one way to be sure that enough people will be present for the groups.

THE UNEDUCATED

Occasionally, moderators are asked to conduct focus groups among target segments composed of people who have not had much formal education. Research among this type of target market does not require dramatic changes from the normal focus group, but there are a few guidelines a moderator should be aware of to maximize the quality of the output from this segment:

- Moderators should recognize that the absence of a formal education does not mean that people are unintelligent. Because a participant is not particularly articulate does not mean that he is not smart, nor does it indicate that he does not have a point of view about specific products and services. Therefore, when working with this type of consumer, it is essential that moderators remain patient, interested, and creative, seeking ways to help participants express their thoughts and feelings. Ultimately, a client's business is affected as much by the reactions of these people as by those of more articulate consumers.

- With a less educated group, it is generally a good idea to use very few (if any) write-down exercises, as the participants might have difficulty with them or take more time than is necessary to write down the information. Further, these people can feel intimidated by the examlike atmosphere that may be communicated by the write-down exercises.

- Generally, less educated groups will require significantly more time to read advertising, concepts, or package copy than would other segments because this population normally does not consider reading skills as important as would a more educated audience. As a result, a moderator should build into the group discussion adequate time for the participants to read and assimilate the information if this type of stimulus is to be part of the group discussion.

SUMMARY

In summary, the principles of conducting focus groups are essentially the same, whether implemented among preteens or older citizens, physicians or the uneducated. However, to maximize the quality of output from segments that are somewhat outside the norm, it is essential that moderators be aware of the guidelines outlined in this chapter. Much of the information is simply common sense. However, other considerations can come only from experience and are integral to the successful implementation of the research. A moderator who follows these guidelines will find that conducting groups with these unique segments will be both productive and rewarding.

15

MODERATING FOCUS GROUPS
INTERNATIONALLY

In the current global economy, companies are placing an increased emphasis on selling products and services to an international market. They seek to build brand equity on a broader scale than ever before to exploit the growing commonalities and benefits from the resultant economies of scale. Most of the companies that now market on a global basis seek a consistent marketing strategy in all countries, with marketing implementation plans that reflect differences in individual countries or geographic areas. This widespread emphasis on global strategies has dramatically expanded the need for marketing research on a worldwide scale. No longer is it sufficient to conduct a study in one country (i.e., the United States) and assume that the research results from this country are projectable to other areas around the world. Similarly, marketing research professionals recognize the need for consistency in the approach to research around the world to ensure that findings can be analyzed within a common framework.

The purpose of this chapter is to present a view of focus group moderating on an international scale so that moderators will understand the options available when proposing a qualitative study that will be conducted in multiple countries. In reading this chapter, it is important to understand that it is not possible to reflect all the nuances of every geographic area relative to the application of qualitative research. To do this would require someone to live and work in each country for an extended period of time. The intent of this material is to alert moderators to the kinds of significant differences that exist in focus group research conducted in the United States and Canada versus other parts of the world so that when the prospect of an international project arises, you will know the questions to ask and be able to anticipate the issues that you are likely to encounter in this type of research.

THE DIFFERENCES BETWEEN QUALITATIVE RESEARCH IN THE UNITED STATES AND ELSEWHERE

There are some significant differences between the United States and almost all other countries (except Canada) with regard to how qualitative research in general and focus groups in particular are conducted. The following will summarize the most important of these differences.

The most obvious difference is one of *language*, as it is generally better to conduct research in the native language of the country. In some industries (i.e., high tech, medical), it may be possible to conduct focus groups in English, as many of the high-level, more educated people working in these industries are fluent in English.

There are also some important *local cultural* issues that must be considered when conducting focus groups outside the United States. This is particularly true in Asia, where the rigid social and professional hierarchy requires that effective groups include people of the same status/level in the same sessions. There are also some issues in various countries regarding the nature of the interaction between the moderator and the participants. For example, whereas U.S. moderators often try to bring some levity to focus groups by joking with participants, some countries would view this as unacceptable, and it might alienate the people in the session from the moderator.

There are some major differences in the *length* of focus groups in the United States and other countries. The typical session in the United States lasts slightly less than 2 hours, whereas it is not unusual for groups in some other countries to be scheduled for 3 to 4 hours. In these groups, there normally are breaks in the sessions, whereas in the United States it is standard procedure to conduct the entire session without any formal breaks.

Another difference between focus groups in the United States and other countries is the *size* of the groups. A typical focus group in the United States includes 8 to 10 people, whereas in many other countries it is not unusual to see groups of only 4 to 6 people. In the United States, this would be considered a mini-group, and it would be the selected option only in certain situations (as outlined in Chapter 1).

When conducting focus groups in the United States, it is standard practice to conduct two or three sessions per day to take advantage of economies of scale. In many countries, it is virtually impossible to conduct more than one focus group per day because of local cultural attitudes regarding going out in the evening, the importance of having dinner with the family unit, or safety concerns about going out after dark to unfamiliar locations.

There are also some significant differences in the *quality of the venues* for focus groups when comparing the United States to foreign countries, but the evidence suggests that this gap is closing each year. Whereas every major city in the United States is likely to have several different focus group facilities with specially constructed one-way mirrors, sensitive sound systems, and hidden cameras, few cities outside the United States and Canada have facilities of this caliber. It is therefore essential that a moderator specify the need for this type of venue when planning sessions outside this country. In many cities throughout the world, focus groups are conducted in

- People's homes, as was done in the United States in the 1960s and 1970s, with the living room used as the group area and a remote camera used in another part of the house as the viewing room

- Small offices that have installed a one-way mirror between two rooms to allow observers to watch from behind the one-way mirror
- Facilities that are more like those in the United States, but without the same type of amenities people expect from American focus group facilities
- There are often lower *levels of professionalism* in the facility staff outside the United States. Though facilities outside the United States can do good work, it is important for moderators to maintain much closer contact with non-U.S. facilities to ensure that:
  — Participants are recruited precisely according to the specifications.
  — Scheduled participants have been confirmed and reconfirmed as part of the overall process so that the requisite number of people come to the groups.
  — The hosting staff understand their responsibilities toward both the client observers and the participants. This includes everything from providing adequate refreshments to both parties, to implementing appropriate rescreening of participants when they arrive, to controlling the noise level outside the room while the group is in session.

There are also some important differences in the *food and drink served to participants* in the United States compared to other countries. For example:

- In many countries, it is common for the participants to be served alcoholic beverages during focus groups. This is not done in the United States except in sessions in which the topic is alcoholic beverages, and in those cases the exposure of the participants to the alcohol is limited because of the facility's liability when the participants leave the groups.
- In many countries, participants are served more substantial food than is typical in the United States, where sandwiches and pizza are almost an industry staple. Further, in other countries, moderators seem more willing to permit eating in the focus group room than is typically allowed in the United States.

Finally, there are some significant differences between the United States and other countries with regard to the *role of the moderator* during the group sessions. In this country, moderators tend to have more struc-tured group sessions, which might explain why they can be imple-mented in 2 hours instead of 3 or 4. A U.S. moderator works within the constraints of the discussion guide and is committed to directing the flow of the conversation. Many foreign moderators tend to be less direc-tive and authoritarian and therefore permit more social conversation and non-project-specific discussion during a session. They also are not as concerned as the U.S. moderator with allowing only one person in the room to talk at a time because they believe that this restriction inhibits the normal flow of human interaction.

IMPLEMENTING INTERNATIONAL RESEARCH

The strategic approach used to execute an international qualitative re-search project can have a major impact on the ultimate quality of the out-put that is generated from the effort. Many client organizations imple-ment global research programs by retaining the services of an international research organization, to which they provide the objectives of the research, the recruitment specifications, a draft discussion guide, and instructions to take the materials and implement the project. In many cases, clients will not even attend the sessions because of the time or expense associated with international research. Although this ap-proach can provide acceptable results, it often lacks some of the basic ele-ments that normally will produce the highest quality global research:

- *The importance of consistency in implementation technique from country to country.* Because the techniques of different moderators around the world can vary widely, the findings could be distorted by a lack of consistency in methodology more than by the substance of the participants' input.
- *The need to have some continuity of representation at the groups.* A sin-gle client should attend all sessions in a project to provide a per-spective on the entire study and to shepherd the process in terms of midstream modifications to the groups, much as the client organi-zation does for domestic groups.
- *The adherence to specific guidelines for reporting the results of the re-search in each country.* This facilitates the analysis of the research in

total and on a country-by-country basis, which is especially important when there are significant differences that need to be understood.

RECOMMENDED APPROACH

We have found that there are two different ways to conduct global focus group research using consistent methodology to produce high-quality outputs.

Consistent Moderator on Site

The optimal approach to global research places the same moderator on site at all facilities. Although this requires some adjustments for language differences (to be discussed below), the benefit of this approach is that the client is assured that a consistent approach to the research is implemented in every market. The implementation of this research involves retaining one moderator to manage the process and to moderate the groups in any markets where English is the native language. The ideal approach is to conduct at least two of the English-speaking groups first so that both the moderator and the client are comfortable with the approach and can make adjustments to the guide, the external stimuli, or the methodology before the study is expanded to other markets.

Once the client and moderator are comfortable with the approach, the moderator travels to each market to meet with the local moderator for several hours. During that time, the moderator presents a tape from the English-speaking groups while the foreign moderator reviews the discussion guide. In this way, the local moderator becomes familiar with the desired approach for the research so that the group is conducted with the same methodology as for all the other groups in the project.

The foreign moderator is also provided with a format for the report that will be written to summarize the groups so that reporting will be consistent across all markets. Focus group moderators who have implemented global studies know that it is always challenging to synthesize the results from many different countries to define overall findings and conclusions. If the inputs from different countries are not provided in a similar format, the task of assimilating all the information becomes even more difficult.

In addition to the pregroup briefing, the moderator attends the groups, watching the sessions via a remote monitor or one-way mirror while a simultaneous translator provides ongoing translations of the discussion. Communication between the local and the coordinating moderators is programmed into the discussion guide so that the foreign moderator will come to the back room every 15 or 20 minutes to ensure that the group is being conducted according to plan. While observing the groups, the moderator will also normally take notes so that these can be compared to the findings and so that conclusions can be developed by the local moderator when they are provided at the conclusion of the study.

This process continues for all markets involved in the study. Though it tends to make the research process take longer and definitely is more expensive than when there is no consistent moderator to manage the process in each market, experience has shown that the quality of the output from the research will more than justify both the extra time and the additional expense.

Moderator Video Record

The second approach is a fallback position from the first and normally occurs when the organization financing the study does not want to spend the money to have a consistent moderator presence in every market or cannot live with the time frame that this approach will normally require. In this situation, the most effective option for implementing the research is as follows:

- The principal moderator (presumably U.S. based) moderates the first two groups, which are conducted in a country where English is appropriate.
- These groups are taped using a camera operator to generate very high-quality tape that can be used for instructional purposes.
- After the groups are completed, the moderator uses the tapes to write a detailed direction document for all foreign moderators that describes each element of the focus group in terms of why the mod-

erator did what he or she did and why it was important to repeat this approach in the local sessions.

- The videotape, direction document, and other key focus group materials are then sent to the moderators in the various countries in advance of the implementation of the groups. This should always be done in time to allow the lead moderator in the United States to communicate with each of the local moderators after they have observed and read the material to address any questions that arise. The personal/telephone contact with the moderator in each of the local countries is very important to the process because it enables the lead moderator to emphasize the key points to the local person who is charged with responsibility for executing the research.

- The lead moderator provides each local moderator with a specific format to use when writing the reports so that reports can be easily summarized and developed into one document.

One way to strengthen this approach to international research is to invest in a videoconferencing service to allow the clients to watch the groups without traveling to the various countries. FocusVision is a videoconferencing company that has relationships with focus group facilities throughout the world and can arrange for a live, remote broadcast of the groups to be transmitted from the country where the sessions are being conducted to the local market in the United States. This gives the moderator the opportunity to manage the process in much the same way as he or she would if local, assuming that appropriate arrangements can be made on one end or the other for simultaneous translation of the material.

Table 15.1 provides a list of research companies that coordinate international assignments.

THE ISSUE OF U.S. MODERATORS
WORKING IN OTHER COUNTRIES

In many international projects, clients ask whether it is appropriate for a U.S. moderator to conduct the groups in a foreign country where English is the native language. The concern is that the difference in accent could

Table 15.1   List of Research Companies That Coordinate International
                  Assignments

Name of Organization	Location	Phone Number
SIS International	Ft. Wayne, IN	(219) 432-2348
Field Facts International	England	011-44-171-736-6990
Research International	England	011-44-171-656-5500
Auton Fiori	England	011-44-171-499-4146
GfK Custom Research	France	011-33-1-47 14 45 27
ICARE	France	011-33-3-20 05 02 50

alienate the local participants, who would prefer to have one of their compatriots implement the work. Further, there are concerns that a moderator from the United States may not be sufficiently comfortable with the nuances of the local country, even if the language is the same, to maximize the effectiveness of moderating. Although I concede that these are legitimate concerns, I believe that the benefits associated with having the lead moderator conduct all the groups that he or she can will more than offset the possible drawbacks. For example:

- Consistency of approach is very important in qualitative research, and there is no better way to have this than to use the same person for all the moderating.
- The potential problems that may be caused by cultural differences can be minimized. An experienced moderator will investigate the local culture and ask the right questions to prepare for the differences and probe them where appropriate for the project. Although the differences cannot be eliminated, they need not pose a major threat to the integrity of the research effort.
- When the number of local moderators is limited, the implementation of international research is simpler and can be better controlled. This reduces the chances for errors, misunderstandings, and discrepancies in findings from the research.
- Finally, we have found that locals in an English-speaking country often prefer to have a U.S. moderator when the project is clearly based in the United States because participants seem to respond enthusiastically to the direct contact this implies with the client company. Personally, I have never felt that the quality of the output

from the participants has suffered when I myself have moderated in another country where the primary language is English.

In summary, conducting global focus group research is different from implementing studies within the United States and Canada. If a moderator charged with managing a global study can understand the most important issues that need to be addressed, the potential problems that can occur in an international study will be dramatically reduced. The most important guideline for the lead moderator is to anticipate problems or issues well in advance of the implementation of the study so that it will be possible to take the actions necessary to complete the assignment successfully.

16

BUILDING A BUSINESS
MODERATING FOCUS GROUPS

To build your own business as a focus group moderator, you will need to use the principles that apply to establishing any business, starting with a business plan that is designed to meet your specific objectives. This section provides guidelines to help you define, plan, create, and sustain a successful business in focus group moderating.

DEVELOPING A VISION

The essential first step in starting a successful business is to clearly differentiate your service from the competition in your category. To this end, you should address the following principles before you begin your own focus group practice.

Identify Your Strengths

You must decide what you have to offer that is different from and, ideally, superior to your competitors. This self-assessment will provide you with the foundation for all the subsequent decisions you make regarding the marketing of your business. Some of the qualities you might examine are

- *Specific category knowledge*, such as prior experience with semiconductors, radio stations, health care, or beauty products. This kind of background can be pivotal when clients are selecting moderators, because some clients feel more confident when they do not need to introduce the moderator to the basic issues that affect their business.
- *Relevant professional experience*, such as psychology, sales, or line marketing. Clients sometimes prefer moderators who have related experience in analyzing and applying the kind of information that is derived from focus groups.
- *Specific demographic experience*, such as prior work in geriatrics, with a certain ethnic group, or with physicians. This is a clear way to carve out a niche in the focus group field.
- *Bilingual capabilities*. As the international marketplace shrinks and more companies seek ways to penetrate more foreign markets, the ability to conduct groups in more than one language becomes increasingly valuable.
- *Educational background in relevant areas*. Some clients appreciate moderators who bring to the project formal advanced training in a field related to the work or an affiliation with an educational institution, which carries the implicit promise that the moderator is current in the field.

Define the Areas Where Your Skills Will Work Best

Determine what kinds of focus groups you will feel most confident and comfortable with and what areas are of greatest interest to you. The list of areas you plan to pursue should reflect what you can offer as a "value-added" service to clients. Your list should be as specific as possible and should cover as broad a range of situations as is appropriate for your skills. These are choices you should consider when determining the types of groups you should and should not moderate:

- Groups with retail consumers versus business-to-business groups
- Groups of professionals, such as physicians, lawyers, architects, or engineers
- Product categories in which you have experience or expertise and those you will not work with for personal reasons, such as tobacco or alcohol
- Demographic groups with whom you will and will not work. You might decide you are not qualified to work with children under 10 or with adults over 65, with various ethnic groups, and so on.

Create Your Positioning

At this point, you should develop a "point of difference" that will distinguish your service from your competition. This is probably the most important part of your marketing plan because it will provide the framework for every proposal you write and help define your approach to every project you undertake. The positioning can be based on prior experience (such as medical, technical, or sales background) that qualifies a moderator for a certain type of clientele. It can be based on a moderator's approach to conducting focus groups, which might be called practical, or theoretical, or participative. A positioning can also be derived from executional considerations such as lower cost, faster work, or more thorough reports. An effective positioning should

- Be unique.
- Provide a meaningful benefit to your prospective clients.
- Be clearly defined.
- Offer long-term possibilities.

Develop a Service Philosophy

Regardless of your positioning, your business should have a foundation of a strong service commitment that should address

- How your clients will be served

- What your pricing policy will be
- How fast you will complete your final reports

GETTING THE WORD OUT

At the start of any business, a formal business plan should be written that will begin with an outline for how to build a client base. Many books have been written to help entrepreneurs write business plans, including my own *Consultant's Manual: A Guide to Building a Successful Consulting Practice*. The details of the business plan are too extensive to cover here, but certain basic elements should be incorporated into the initial planning for a business in focus group research.

The first step in launching your business is to generate awareness of your service among your target audience. If potential clients become aware of your name and service over time, they will be receptive to your proposals for specific work, and they will be more willing to accept a referral by a colleague. This means that ongoing periodic exposure to your business and name is essential to your long-term success.

There are two primary ways for service organizations to build awareness of themselves: direct targeted contact and indirect methods that establish a presence. You should use both approaches if your business is to thrive.

Direct Methods

The three principal methods that moderators use to market their practice are direct mail, telemarketing, and advertising.

Direct Mail

This medium is the most frequently used way that service companies build awareness of their services. It is relatively inexpensive and can be targeted specifically to the people who are the best prospects for their services. There are several types of direct mail solicitations, each with its own advantages and drawbacks.

The first is *cold call letters* that are sent to a targeted list of prospective clients who meet criteria that the moderator has established. These letters will usually be sent to a list of market research directors in companies that use focus groups, and they will sometimes include a brochure introducing the research company's services. The letter is designed to pave the way for the client to consider the moderator when the next focus group project arises. Despite the widespread use of cold call letters, they are not always effective because clients often see them as junk mail and discard them. Nonetheless, repeated mailings over time, especially if there is a clear point of difference that jumps out, can result in a level of awareness that will make your name spring to mind the next time a client you have targeted is considering doing focus groups.

A more effective form of direct mail is the *quasi-cold call letter*, which introduces some frame of reference for the contact. It is a targeted mailing to people who have some knowledge of the sender or of a third party who endorses the sender. If an existing client, a friend, a business associate, or some other contact gives you the names of some prospective clients, you can write them a letter saying that the contact suggested you communicate with them about the services you offer. This approach dramatically increases the chances that the targeted client will read your letter.

Whether you use one or both forms of direct mail letters, you must follow them up with a telephone call if you hope to generate a real lead. It is unlikely that the target will be the one to pursue you. With this type of effort, you have the advantage of controlling the timing of the mailing to orchestrate manageable periods of follow-up contact.

Telemarketing

A second direct method of building awareness is telemarketing. Like direct mail, this can be cold calls or third-party referenced calls. Telemarketing has two advantages over direct mail. The first is that the personal contact affords you the opportunity to answer questions the client may have and to try to set up a meeting where you can present your credentials, establish rapport, and maybe even discuss a specific project.

Another advantage of telemarketing is that you can control the timing and number of calls you make at any given time. This means that during periods of intense commitments to existing clients, you can focus single-mindedly on the work at hand, using the inevitable future downtime to place phone calls.

Telemarketing does have disadvantages. It can be very time consuming, especially when secretaries or other intermediaries are involved or when clients are repeatedly unavailable. Using telemarketing can have the added drawback of its expense, especially when long-distance calls are involved.

Advertising

The third direct method of building awareness is through paid advertising in newspapers, magazines, trade show or conference brochures, and other vehicles. Advertising can be an excellent approach if the following guidelines are followed:

- The message should be a meaningful, easy-to-understand, and unique statement of your positioning or point of difference.
- You should select specific media capable of reaching a large percentage of your target audience, defined as the primary prospects for your service.
- You must spend enough money in your selected media to reach your target audience with sufficient frequency to register effectively your company name and message (i.e., reason to use *your* service). In general, it is considered adequate to reach the audience four times over a 6-month period.

Paid advertising is also an effective way to reach your target audience in an appropriate environment. An adequate frequency supporting the right message can make a lasting impression. The cost, however, can be considerable, and if your budget cannot support appropriate levels, it is more efficient to turn to other means of getting your message out.

Indirect Methods

Whether used alone or in conjunction with direct methods, indirect approaches to building awareness differ from the direct approaches discussed above in several respects:

- They generally require significant amounts of your time but not a meaningful financial investment.
- You do not have as much control over the outcome of your indirect efforts as you would over direct activities.
- The marketing focus of indirect methods is likely to be on long-term awareness building rather than achieving immediate name recognition as a result of the activities.

There are four principal indirect methods of building awareness: public relations, publishing, teaching and seminars, and community involvement.

Public Relations

Public relations includes all activities that are covered in media that reach your target customers. One of the best ways to use public relations is to get quoted as an expert in a story in trade publications that reach your target. These publications are generally read thoroughly by the appropriate people, who are actively looking for relevant information in their industry and who are likely to take note of experts who might be able to help them. Other ways of getting your name into the media in objective, authoritarian environments are:

- Conduct a focus group without charge for a volunteer organization such as the United Way, the Red Cross, or your town government. Contact your local newspaper, TV station, or radio station to see if you can interest them in the work and findings.
- Become involved in a trade organization, either in marketing research or in a specific industry. Offer to conduct a focus group among the members to identify trends in the industry. Trade publications like to publish this type of information, as it is of interest to all of their members.
- Cultivate a relationship with the local or trade press, and try to get them to cover any speeches you give, positions you accept in trade or community organizations, courses you teach at the local high school or college, and so forth.

Where public relations is involved, you must always be thinking about ways to interest the press in your activities so it will cover your efforts. You must view this as a long-term effort, but one that can be very beneficial in building awareness and generating leads over time.

Publishing

One of the best ways to build awareness of your business is to publish articles about topics related to focus groups in appropriate publications, both horizontal and vertical. Horizontal publications are not industry specific but are aimed at marketing managers, marketing research professionals, or ad agency account executives in any industry that might be interested in considering the use of your services. Vertical publications are industry specific and include titles such as *Bank Marketing, Television/Radio Age,* and *PC Week.* These types of publications reach people at all levels and in different functional areas within the companies in the particular industry. Publishing articles in both types of publications is an excellent way to become known in your industry and to build your reputation as an expert. Further, your published articles can be used as direct mail inserts or as leave-behinds after meetings or focus group sessions and can be helpful in differentiating you from others in the field.

For publishing to be an effective tool, you must commit yourself to getting articles published four to six times per year, and you should submit your work to several different publications to increase the chances that your articles will run.

Teaching and Seminars

Another indirect route to making clients aware of you is to teach a course in marketing research at a local adult education program or nearby university. This gives you exposure as an expert to students who are often working for companies (full or part time) that might need your services. Participation in trade meetings and conventions as a speaker or a panelist is also an excellent way to obtain exposure to potential clients in a very appropriate environment.

Community Involvement

If you become involved in community organizations, you can gain exposure to potential clients, who often volunteer their time locally. The semisocial environment of such organizations gives you access to people you might otherwise have difficulty reaching. Try to contribute to the organization something related to marketing and/or focus groups so that the other people will appreciate your professional capabilities. This is not a forum for selling your services or generating leads, but rather a place where your name and expertise establish themselves in the community.

Indirect methods of building awareness offer two important advantages over direct methods: There is virtually no financial commitment, and you build credibility as an expert while you are building awareness. On the negative side, you do not have control over the frequency, timing, and content of the messages that result because it is difficult to determine when or if you will get coverage in the press, whether your articles will be published, or when you might be a selected speaker. The work you do to gain exposure can be very time consuming, but the impact can be enormous.

Using the Internet

Somewhere between direct and indirect communication efforts is the Internet. The fastest-growing approach to selling a service is through Web sites. Your Web site is like a storefront, and it must work to lure people "in" and then tell them the most important and relevant information about you and your company. It has been my experience that one of the most fertile sources of new business over the past 2 years has been inquiries received via my Web site (www.groupsplus.com). For the Web site to work effectively for you, it must have the following:

- A way for prospective clients to find the site as a result of going into a search engine to learn about qualitative research.
- An interesting and appealing format so that visitors who get to your site are interested enough to surf around it in order to see what you have included.
- Some helpful information they can download, in order to give them a tangible benefit from their visit to your site. In my company Web site, we have an easy way for visitors to download dozens of

articles I have written about focus groups and an extensive bibliography of other articles that are available but not for downloading.

- An easy vehicle for visitors to contact you if they want more information or wish to discuss a potential project with you.

In summary, I found my investment in our Web site to be one of the best business decisions I have ever made: Not only is it a helpful sales tool, but it can be a very effective way to provide interested parties with information about your company on an immediate basis without having to resort to faxes or expensive overnight messenger services.

SELLING YOUR SERVICES

No matter what your marketing program, if you are not able to sell your service to a prospective client, all the recognition you have gained for your company will have been wasted. Whether you consider yourself a salesperson or not, your success as a focus group moderator will be directly proportional to your effectiveness as a salesperson. The selling of focus group services involves three key elements—generating qualified leads, presenting your credentials to prospects, and writing proposals, all of which need to be executed very effectively if you are to be successful. The following provides a brief discussion of each.

Generating Leads

A successful focus group business will have three ongoing sources of qualified leads: the direct and indirect awareness-building tactics discussed above, satisfied clients, and relationships with facilities. If you have implemented a strong awareness-building marketing effort, you should have an important source of leads already in place.

The most valuable source of leads for your business is your satisfied clients. Once they know and appreciate the quality of your work and the scope of your service, clients become excellent sources of repeat business, often using a focus group moderator as a regular consultant to their business who conducts all qualitative research for them. In addition, a satisfied client is usually quite willing to refer your services to a colleague or other clients.

Another fertile source of leads is local focus group research facilities with whom you have a good working relationship. It is in your best interest to establish good relationships with these organizations, as they are often asked for references of qualified moderators to assist them in planning and implementing an assignment. It is best to identify the facilities that you will be using regularly and to concentrate as much business as possible with them. Not only will they become a source of business for you, but they will also work to serve you and your clients better.

Presenting Your Credentials

Once you have been invited to present your credentials, you should make the most of this opportunity to sell your services, capabilities, background, and initial thoughts for their project if you know what they are trying to evaluate in advance of your presentation. The most important part of your credentials presentation is your account of the "unique point of difference" that you offer relative to your competition, as outlined earlier in this chapter. Your positioning should be the focus of your presentation, with all other aspects of your presentation supporting this point of difference. The ideal presentation of your focus group credentials should contain the following:

- *An overview of the services you provide*—This should identify the various services you provide, including such activities as the selection of the facility, coordinating with the facilities, recruiting the participants, development of the discussion guide, moderating the groups, presentation of a final report, and perhaps preparation of written transcripts of the session.
- *Your background and credentials*—This involves communicating the key elements from your resume, including your education, job history, other experience related to the prospect's needs, publications, and key positions you have held in relevant industry groups.
- *Your unique point of difference*—This is the positioning of your company, articulated in a way that identifies the most important message about your services that differentiates you from the competition.

- *Your approach to moderating*—This includes general costs, scheduling, and your relationship with facilities. It is not possible to provide prospective clients with a "rate card" for focus groups, but there are some meaningful points that you can communicate, such as the range of cost for your groups and the timing.
- *Your previous clients and category experience*—It is important to communicate the different types of assignments you have had and clients you have served. To some prospective clients, this is the most important part of any credentials presentation because it helps them see whether you are a seasoned professional.

Your presentation should be flexible in format, allowing for and accommodating a one-on-one meeting in addition to a small group if necessary. Most people will develop a computer-generated presentation using a program such as Powerpoint or Freelance to make it more interesting and persuasive. If this is done properly, it will add significant credence to the professionalism you are trying to communicate to the prospect organization. You should have available a brief summary of your presentation to leave with your potential client after the presentation. This should include relevant attachments such as articles you have published or press coverage you have received, as these will add to your professional credentials.

Writing Proposals

Once you have been briefed on a specific project that you will be bidding on, the next step will be to write a formal proposal. The elements that should be included in this proposal are covered in Chapter 6.

SERVICING CLIENTS

Developing good client relationships is fundamental to the creation of a thriving focus group business. Clients are an excellent source of repeat business and also are often the sources of productive referrals, as we discussed relative to building awareness. In many cases, the most successful and productive client relationships result largely from the service component of the business. Though many moderators are capable of moderating effectively and writing excellent reports, these same people often overlook the importance of customer service in building effective and long-lasting relationships. The key components of good customer service are as follows.

Personal Involvement

A key component of effective client service is to get to know the people involved in your project at the client organization. This will differentiate you from the pool of focus group "vendors" who serve the client. Some degree of personal relationship is particularly reassuring to clients when you are their eyes, ears, and voice on the other side of the one-way mirror. This does not mean that you do extensive entertaining but rather that you take a genuine interest in your clients as people and perhaps occasionally interact with them in a relaxed environment. The traveling involved in focus group projects will often create excellent opportunities for you to interact with your clients, which is another good reason to have a positive relationship with them.

Regular Contact

You should maintain contact with your clients throughout the focus group process to keep them up to date on all important details, especially when recruiting is underway and the progress is a fundamental determinant of whether the groups will be implemented as planned. As indicated in a prior chapter, often recruiting specifications will need to be changed while the recruiting is happening in order to fill the groups. The decisions relative to changing the specifications of the participants should be made in conjunction with the client to ensure that they are in agreement with the modifications.

Availability

One of the greatest complaints that clients have about moderators is that they are not available to talk to them when they call. A client should never have to wait more than half a day for you to return a phone call. In addition to being accessible for questions about the process, you have to be willing to juggle your own schedule to meet the client's needs for the groups, the briefing session, and the presentation of the final report.

Speed

Focus groups are often selected as a research methodology because they are a fast way to get information. Clients turn to focus groups frequently as a way to get answers that will allow them to move rapidly to the next step in their marketing process. This means that a sense of urgency on the part of the moderator, from planning and scheduling the groups through the delivery of the final report, is likely to indicate to your clients that you are the right person for the job. As a general rule, I complete the final report within 5 days of the final session.

MEASURING CLIENT SATISFACTION

Moderators who pay attention to their clients' needs and are good at their work generally also pay attention to how clients assess their work. Nonetheless, I strongly recommend that moderators use a formal system to monitor how satisfied their clients are. An excellent way to evaluate this is to send a brief questionnaire to your client immediately after the completion of a focus group project.

The questionnaire should ask for an assessment of the following areas:

- Overall satisfaction (5-point scale)
- The moderator guide
- The moderation of the groups
- The performance of the facility with regard to recruitment, physical plant, and food
- The quality of the final report
- The timing of the groups and the report
- Suggested ways to increase client satisfaction with the total process

In summary, both the challenges and benefits of having your own business in focus group research are great. If you plan to pursue such a career move, be sure to start with a thorough, distinctive marketing plan, and then follow your plan every step of the way. Adhering to the principles outlined in this chapter will help you succeed in your business for a long and gratifying time.

17

PRICING FOCUS GROUPS

There is an old saying that "nothing happens until a sale is made." This is clearly the case in the focus group business. A moderator who does not sell projects will not have a business unless the selling is done by someone else in the organization, with the moderator responsible only for the facilitation and reporting of the research. However, the majority of people who work full time in the focus group moderation business are entrepreneurs who own their business and rely on their ability to sell to keep the organization functioning.

A vital part of the selling process in the focus group industry is the pricing of projects. If an assignment is priced too low, the research company will not make sufficient profits to make the business viable. On the other hand, if the project is priced too high, it is unlikely that the project will be accepted by the ultimate client. Therefore, it is essential that a moderator understand both the philosophy of pricing and how to most effectively implement a pricing strategy in the company so that it contributes to a positive financial situation for the organization. The purpose of this chapter is to discuss the philosophy of pricing focus group projects, provide an approach to costing an assignment, and share some thoughts on billing and collections.

THE PHILOSOPHY OF PRICING

There are basically four approaches to pricing focus group assignments: pricing to a margin, pricing to standard costs, pricing to the market, and pricing to a client.

Pricing to a Margin

One approach used by many companies is to develop their pricing on the basis of a margin that is considered to be acceptable for the financial stability of the organization. To implement this approach, the company determines the out-of-pocket costs for the assignment (i.e., those that must be paid out to cover the facility charges, recruiting, and participant honoraria) and then multiplies these by a factor that has been determined on the basis of the margin the moderator has established for the business. For example, if the out-of-pocket costs for an assignment come in at $12,650, the moderator multiplies this amount by the standard escalator used in his or her practice (e.g., 2.1) to arrive at a project cost of $26,565, which would return a margin of 52.4%.

Pricing to Standard Costs

This is an approach to pricing whereby the moderator determines the out-of-pocket costs the same way as in the pricing-to-margin approach and then adds to this the various costs that are involved in the assignment. These would include some or all of the following:

- Development of the discussion guide
- Field supervision (e.g., facility management, screener development)
- Moderating
- Report writing
- Report presentation

The approach to costing individual elements such as development of the discussion guide, moderating, and report writing will vary by moderator. I have always followed the approach that the costs for these elements are based on the average amount of time that they take to complete, and this time is multiplied by an hourly rate that I charge for my services. Over time, we have established a standard rate for such services as development of the guide, moderating two groups on the same day, and the report, as the time does not vary dramatically for them on a project-by-project basis. This makes the costing of focus group projects much easier, as we do not have to go through the hourly calculation each time.

When these costs are added to the out-of-pocket expenses, the moderator arrives at a price that will be charged to the client.

Pricing to the Market

This is an approach to pricing whereby the research company calculates its costs on the basis of the standard pricing formula described above and then adjusts the actual price to be charged the prospective client on the basis of what the market will bear. In essence, the philosophy behind this approach is that the price of the assignment depends on what the moderator feels will be accepted by the prospective client, which can result in a reduction or an increase in the absolute margin that will be generated by the project.

This approach assumes that the moderator has a very good understanding of the prevailing costs in the industry and for the specific business type where the proposal has been sent, so that the adjusted pricing will work to the benefit of the research company. It also assumes that the moderator will be willing to work for lower than the standard cost formula if that is necessary to get the assignment.

Pricing to a Client

This approach to pricing is relevant only when the moderator has an established relationship with a client. The philosophy of this approach is to price to a level that will be acceptable to the client while at the same time providing an adequate return to the researcher. Many focus group moderators feel that they are best served by keeping the costs of "like" assignments in a very similar range in the same client organization in order to minimize the impact that the price is likely to have on whether the assignment is accepted. This may require the moderator to accept a lower margin on some assignments than others and also can make it difficult to reflect real price increases in field costs. However, with established clients, it may be worthwhile to sacrifice some short-term profits in order to retain the long-term relationship.

HANDLING ANCILLARY FOCUS GROUP COSTS

In all focus group assignments, additional costs (both soft and hard) are incurred during the course of the assignment. The purpose of this section is to identify the most common charges that are incurred and how they might be handled by the moderator relative to the ultimate pricing of the assignment. Specifically, the following additional costs are frequently incurred during the execution of a focus group assignment.

Travel Expenses

These are the costs associated with the moderator's travel to and from the group locations. Normally, these are billed separately as expenses, without a markup. Some organizations feel a need to mark up these expenses by 7% to 15% in order to cover the handling costs associated with making the reservations and carrying the expenses until reimbursement. My bias is to bill expenses at cost and assume that the handling and carrying charges are built into the cost of doing business.

Taping

It is standard practice in the industry to provide audiotapes free of charge as part of the overall facility costs. Some facilities will also provide videotaping free (with a fixed camera only) as part of the services provided, whereas others will charge a nominal fee for video to recover their investment costs associated with the camera. Occasionally a client feels a need to have a higher quality tape and requests a camera operator to film the groups in order to make the video more interesting and easier to view by others in the client organization or to use segments of the group in an internal meeting. The use of a camera operator is relatively expensive, normally at least $250+ per group.

It is my strong recommendation that out-of-pocket costs associated with taping be charged at cost, directly to the client. If the moderator is not charged for a standing videotape, then the client should not have to pay for this service.

Food

There are two components of focus group food, which are normally handled very differently relative to the charging to clients. Specifically:

- Food served to participants (meals or snacks) is normally included as a part of the facility charges and should be part of a "standard costing" formula. As a result, the client organization is charged for the meals but only as part of the overall facility costs.
- Food served to the client observers who watch the groups from the back room is a different matter. The quality of this food is normally considerably higher (and therefore more expensive) than food served to the participants. Further, at the time a proposal is being developed, the moderator does not know if 2 or 20 clients will be attending the sessions, so it is impossible to estimate accurately the costs that will be incurred for client food. Therefore, I am strongly in favor of unbundling this cost and charging the client for the actual expenses incurred, based on the number of observers who come to the groups. In my opinion, it is not appropriate for a moderator to mark up these expenses, as it is a service to the client organization for which the moderator did not have to incur costs.

Sales Taxes

Rather than trying to practice law or accounting, I simply want to alert the reader to the sales tax issue. The laws are different in various states, and the interpretation of the need to charge sales taxes does differ. The important consideration is that the moderator be aware of the issues relative to sales taxes; otherwise, he or she may be unpleasantly surprised with a tax bill that probably will not be collectable from past clients.

Ancillary Services Provided by the Facility

There are situations in which a client is in need of special services to be performed by a focus group facility, such as purchasing competitive products or renting special equipment to be used in the groups. These expenses should be identified in a focus group proposal as rebillable to the client at the cost that is charged by the facility to the moderator.

NEGOTIATING WITH CLIENTS

It is not uncommon in the focus group industry for a client to attempt to negotiate the pricing of a proposal with a focus group moderator in order to reduce the costs of the research effort. I feel very strongly that negotiations with clients relative to fees are not appropriate for a moderator to engage in under any circumstances, for two key reasons:

1. If a price can be negotiated, the implication is that there is extra margin in the pricing formula, possibly suggesting that the moderator is charging too much for his or her services. This is not an image that I feel most moderators would like to have with their clients.

2. If a moderator negotiates with a client on a project, it is virtually certain that this will establish a precedent that will result in negotiations for every assignment that is proposed by the moderator.

How then, can a moderator deal with a client's request to reduce the cost of a proposal without compromising the pricing policy or the integrity of the organization? We find that the best approach to this situation is to offer the client the option of one or more of the following:

- A reduction in the number of people who will be recruited for each group, which will save both recruiting funds and co-op payments to the participants. Often, this can generate enough of a savings to satisfy the needs of the client.
- A different type of report that will be less costly. For example, perhaps a top-line summary will be adequate rather than a full moderator report. This can result in meaningful savings, particularly for small assignments.
- An attempt to recruit the groups with a lower than normal co-op cost. This is the most risky of the three alternatives, as it could end up being the more expensive alternative if the lower co-op requires more time in the recruitment process, thereby resulting in higher charges from the facility to get people who will come to the groups at the lower rate.

BILLING AND COLLECTIONS

Whereas "nothing happens until a sale is made" is certainly an important statement about the selling process, the bottom line of running a focus group moderating business is getting paid for the services performed. The focus group business is such that a bad debt can have significant implications for the business because approximately half of all costs that are included in a project are out-of-pocket expenses, most of which need to be paid out to the facility in advance of the groups. Therefore, if an account becomes uncollectable, the moderator has lost both the out-of-pocket expenses and also the time charges associated with planning and implementing the groups.

Another aspect of this issue is cash flow, which can be a major problem in this industry because of the long payment cycles of many clients and the need to pay facilities up front in order to implement the groups. As a result, it is not unusual for a moderator to complete an assignment before receiving any money, even though he or she has paid out half the value of the project to the focus group facility. This can create such a serious cash flow deficit that a moderator can seriously jeopardize his or her ability to continue to do business, for facilities will not want to set up groups for moderators who do not pay their bills.

In view of the payment and collection issues and the major implications that these can have for a focus group business, we have found the following to be reasonable ways to address these potential problems so that they do not threaten the viability of the business:

- *Check out the prospective client*—One of the biggest mistakes that some focus group moderators make is working for whoever offers to pay for a project. Sometimes the intent to pay has no connection with delivery of the check. This is particularly true with regard to start-up companies that are relying on investment monies to pay the development/research costs. Therefore, it is strongly suggested that the moderator perform due diligence relative to new clients with the goal of trying to determine their ability to pay. This could include obtaining bank references and vendor references.

- *Insist on receiving an advance payment*—Many focus group moderators will ask for 50% of the project fee upon approval in order to cover the out-of-pocket costs, most of which must be paid before the research company receives its final check. Although this is a very good policy in theory, in practice it is almost impossible to enforce, particularly when one is working with large corporations. This is because the procurement process in big companies often involves the development of purchase orders and then the movement of purchase orders through the system. Further, some companies have developed a policy in which they will pay their "vendors" in 45 days (or even more), recognizing that this creates cash flow problems for the people with whom they do business. However, for a large company, the lengthening of payment time results in meaningful incremental revenues, which the vice president of finance can claim represent incremental bottom-line profits for the corporation. Unfortunately, few companies place more than cursory attention to the implications of this practice for the relationships with suppliers and the general financial health of the organizations who provide the needed services to the client company.

- *Take a very aggressive posture toward collections*—Many small business people have difficulty asking customers for money, as they feel it will threaten their relationship. However, we have found that it is much better to pursue companies to get paid than to wait unnecessarily long times for payment, which probably will create anger and anxiety on the part of the research company. Often the collection of payments can be handled between the moderator and the accounts payable department in the company, which can facilitate the process of getting paid without creating potential problems with the key people in the client organization who will be responsible for hiring your company to implement the next assignment.

SUMMARY

In summary, moderators should remember that few people are in the market research business only for fun and that profitability is an important part of staying in business. Therefore, it is imperative that moderators develop a pricing strategy for the business that will provide them with an approach to costing out assignments consistently. Further, it is essential that moderators carefully evaluate the variable costs of focus groups and be sure to unbundle them so that they do not get out of control and eat into the profitability of an assignment. Finally, the billing and collections process is essential to the long-term viability of any research company, and the owner of the research company must ensure that adequate attention is paid to this area. If the company does not get paid, it will no longer be a company!

GLOSSARY

Anthropomorphization—A moderation technique in which participants describe a product or service in terms of a human being. The objective of this vehicle is to permit the moderator to probe the participants' feelings about the product or service by giving the inanimate object life, personality, and a lifestyle.

At-home testing—A procedure in which participants are provided with a product sample to use at home before a group session so that they will be more knowledgeable about it and better prepared to discuss it during the session. The procedure can also be used after a session, when a product sample is provided to participants with the agreement that they will be telephoned to follow up on their reaction to the item.

Attitudinal scaling—A moderation technique that focuses on the two most important characteristics of a product or service. Participants are instructed to conceptualize the product or service on a two-dimensional scale, such as price and quality, side effects and efficacy, or speed and cost. This helps the moderator delve deeper into the participants' feelings about the product or service.

Audiotaping—The audiotape recording of focus group proceedings. Virtually all group sessions are audiotaped.

Back room—The observation room from which client personnel watch and listen to focus group proceedings through a one-way mirror.

Bid—The estimate a facility provides to a client or moderator, covering the cost of the group session(s). Normally a bid includes the cost of recruiting, co-op payments, room rental, and food. A moderator's charge for conducting focus groups could also be a bid. The term *bid* usually involves getting prices from different suppliers for a particular job.

Briefing—A meeting in which a client provides a moderator with sufficient background information about a research project so that the moderator can recommend the most appropriate research methodology and, if focus groups are called for, begin to prepare for them. A briefing may be either face-to-face interaction or a telephone conversation.

Co-op—The payment provided to participants as an incentive to come to the focus groups. The amount varies dramatically depending on the difficulty of recruiting the participants. This is also called the honorarium, particularly for medical or professional focus groups.

Cold call—A selling situation in which the salesperson makes contact with a prospective client without any prior introduction. It can be in the form of a direct mail letter, a broadcast fax or e-mail, or a personal call. Generally, the sales effectiveness of cold calls in service business is very limited.

Concept board—A visual aid (external stimuli) used in a focus group to present an idea to the participants so that they can react to it as part of the group discussion. Normally a concept board consists of a brief description of the idea, often presented with a visual in order to make it more realistic to the participants in the group.

Concept statement—A brief description of a new product, service or promotion event intended to provide participants in a focus group with sufficient information so that they can make a judgment as to the absolute value of the concept and its most important strengths and limitations.

Conceptual mapping—A moderation technique in which participants are asked to place the names of products or services on a grid. How they group the items on the diagram is used to stimulate discussion.

Conclusions—The section of the final report that contains the moderator's interpretation of the output from the group sessions in light of the research objectives.

Conjoint association—A moderation technique in which participants are asked to choose between two hypothetical products or services, each of which has different attributes. The objective is to stimulate discussion about the various attributes in order to gain insight into the relative value of each.

Database—The computerized list of people whom a facility has identified as willing to participate in a session sometime in the future. Normally, a database contains basic demographic data (e.g., age, income, and occupation) and selective product usage information. This enables the facility to recruit qualified persons for focus group sessions relatively easily. The number of people listed varies dramatically, but most facilities in metropolitan areas have over 5,000 names from which they can provide "fresh," qualified respondents.

Demographics—The objective and quantifiable characteristics of consumers by which they are classified into groups. Demographic designators include age, marital status, income, family size, and occupation, among many others.

Discussion guide—see **Guide.**

Duplicate number validation—An emerging service in the focus group industry in which the names and telephone numbers of people recruited for groups are submitted to a central screening organization *in advance* of the groups for the purpose of screening out people who have recently participated in any session or are involved in focus groups more frequently than is desired.

Dyad—A qualitative research methodology in which an interviewer works with two participants at once. This technique is particularly appropriate for products and services for which two persons are relatively equal partners in making a purchase decision.

Expressive drawing—A moderation technique in which participants are asked to express their reaction to a product or service by drawing a picture.

External stimuli—Objects that are introduced into a focus group to generate reactions from the participants. Examples include concept boards, product prototypes, and rough and finished advertising.

Facility—The organization in whose physical plant the focus groups are held. The traditional setup is a room with a large conference table that seats 10 people comfortably and an observation room, which are connected to each other by a one-way mirror. A facility also normally provides a variety of services such as recruiting the participants, providing food, procuring competitive product samples, and arranging for the videotaping of the sessions.

Field service—Another term for **Facility,** except that not many field services also do quantitative surveys via telephone.

Final report—The document that the moderator develops at the conclusion of focus group sessions. Its length varies, but a typical final report has several sections: a summary of the methodology used in the groups, a review of the key findings, and the conclusions or the moderator's *interpretation* of what the findings mean in light of the research objectives. Some final reports also have a recommendations section, which contains the moderator's suggestions for the next steps that the client should take based on the conclusions of the research.

Findings—The portion of the final report in which the "facts" from the focus groups are summarized. This section is normally organized along the lines of the moderator guide and covers each of the topics identified in it. It does not interpret the information but reports the findings on which the interpretation will be based.

Fixed personality association—A projective moderation technique in which participants are shown pictures of people, places, or things and asked to interpret them with regard to the topic. Fixed personality associations use the same pictures over an extended period of time rather than varying them, thus creating "norms" that may apply to a large number of sessions.

Focus group—A qualitative market research technique in which a group of 8 to 10 participants of common demographics, attitudes, or purchase patterns are led through a (usually) 2-hour discussion of a particular topic by a trained moderator.

Focus Vision—A company headquartered in Stamford, Connecticut that operates a network of focus group facilities offering live remote broadcasting and two-way communication between a facility and a client's office. This service enables client organizations to observe groups in various parts of the country without having to travel.

"Fresh" participants—Persons who have never participated in a session previously or have not done so for several years.

Full group—A focus group with 8 to 10 participants. A less than full group is normally referred to as a mini-group.

Global focus—Focus groups conducted using satellite video technology in which participants are located in different places, normally in different countries.

Grid—A graphic provided to focus group participants in conceptual mapping and attitudinal scaling exercises.

Group dynamics—The impact of participants' inputs on one another in a focus group discussion. An effective moderator, using group dynamics techniques, can promote helpful discussion and also minimize the potentially negative effects of group dynamics.

GroupNet—A trade name for the Video Conferencing Alliance Network, which is a group of field services that offers videoconferencing of focus groups.

Guide—The outline that the moderator uses to lead the discussion in the focus group session. It is also called the moderator guide. It is developed by the moderator on the basis of the briefing and identifies the topics that will be covered in a focus group session and the approximate emphasis given to each. This is the primary way the moderator communicates with the client organization about the anticipated content of the focus group session.

Homogeneous groups—Focus groups in which the participants have extremely similar characteristics.

Honorarium—The co-op payment provided to focus group participants. The term *honorarium* is most frequently used when the participants are professionals, such as physicians, lawyers, and architects.

Host/hostess—The individual (male or female) responsible for greeting the participants as they arrive at the facility and for preparing the room. Responsibilities include providing food for the participants and the client observers, rescreening respondents when they arrive, and preparing name tags.

In-house recruiting—The recruiting of participants by telephone solicitations from people physically located within the focus group facility. Most moderators prefer in-house recruiting because it allows them more control over the recruiting process.

Incentive—The co-op payment to participants for coming to a focus group.

Incidence—The percentage of people in a population who qualify for a focus group, based on the specifications that have been developed. The higher the incidence, the less expensive it is to recruit participants for a focus group.

Intercept—A recruitment method in which an interviewer stops (or "intercepts") people in a mall or other public location and asks them a brief series of screening questions.

Intro board—This is a visual aid used in the beginning of a focus group to help with the introduction of the participants to each other, the moderator, and the client observers in the back room. Normally, it provides direction to the participants to provide information such as their first name, family composition, and occupation. An example of an intro board is provided in Figure G.1.

Laddering—A probing technique, used in one-on-ones and focus groups, designed to delve into the "real" reasons for participants' behavior and attitudes toward the topic. It is generally considered an intensive technique, as it probes in-depth each topic that is discussed in such a way as to try to get to the underlying reason for the attitude or behavior. The moderator seeks the reason behind each answer until he or she arrives at a basic human need such as ego or status.

Lists—Names of customers, former customers, suppliers, or industry influentials that clients sometimes provide to interviewers, from which participants are to be recruited for focus groups.

FIRST NAME

OCCUPATION

COMPANY NAME

FAMILY COMPOSITION

Figure G.1. A Sample Intro Board

Mall intercept—see **Intercept.**

Methodology—The section of the final report in which the moderator outlines the approach used in the research, including the method of recruiting participants, the location of the groups and the external stimuli used. *Methodology* can also mean the approach that a moderator uses to conduct the sessions.

Mini-group—A focus group that contains four to six participants. More than six is normally considered a "full group," and fewer than four is a triad or a dyad.

Mixed group—A focus group that contains both males and females. Most moderators prefer to work with groups that are not mixed.

Moderator guide—see **Guide.**

No-show—A focus group participant who agrees to come to a session and is confirmed the same day but nonetheless does not come to the group. Facilities attempt to compensate for the problem caused by no-shows by overrecruiting for the group by two or three people per session.

Notes—The summary information that observers develop during focus groups. Normally, notes are only their most important comments written in a shorthand format.

Observation room—see **Back room.**

One-on-one—A qualitative research technique in which a moderator interviews one participant, normally for 30 to 60 minutes. Often this is conducted in a room with a one-way mirror so the client can observe the proceedings.

Overrecruiting—Selecting the extra people for a focus group to compensate for the inevitable "no-shows."

Participant—A person who takes part in a focus group.

People board—A moderation technique in the class of fixed personality associations, developed by Tom Greenbaum. Participants are exposed to a permanent display of photographs of people of various ages, socioeconomic levels, and ethnic groups that enables the moderator to delve further into the thoughts and feelings of the participants about the topic being discussed. The advantage of this fixed personality association over variable personality associations is that norms of participants' reactions to each image are established over time, thereby helping the moderator to interpret participants' reactions and indicating areas to probe during the discussions.

"Professional" respondent—A participant who attends many sessions by volunteering for the recruitment lists of different facilities. Most moderators seek to eliminate "professional" respondents from groups because they do not generally respond in the same objective way that "fresh" respondents do but try to anticipate what they think moderators want to hear.

Projectability—The capacity of research results to be extrapolated to the larger universe on the assumption that the sample is representative of the total. Focus groups are sometimes criticized because, as a qualitative methodology, their results are not projectable due to the small samples involved and the selectiveness of participant recruitment.

Projective—A class of moderation techniques used to stimulate discussion among participants. These techniques force the participants to think about the topic in a more subjective or creative way than they might in a "normal" discussion. Projectives include sentence completion, expressive drawing, anthropomorphization, and associations.

Qualitative research—Research whose objective is to gain insight into attitudes and feelings, not to develop numerical data that may be projectable to a larger universe. Qualitative methodologies include focus groups, mini-groups, and one-on-ones.

Quantitative research—Research designed to generate projectable numerical data about a topic. Quantitative studies are conducted by telephone, mail, or personal interviews.

Quota—A minimum number of focus group participants who must meet certain criteria. A moderator might set a quota of having half of the group be users of Brand X or one third be aware of Product Y.

Random selection—A selection process in which everyone has an equal chance of being chosen for participation. Random recruiting is the ideal for respondents for both qualitative and quantitative studies. But due to cost considerations, only a small percentage of all quantitative research conducted uses purely random sampling. For focus group sessions, recruitment is almost never random.

Rating—A technique used in focus groups aimed primarily at identifying the overall attitudes of the participants toward a specific topic. Each individual is asked to rate the idea on a 10-point scale, and the moderator uses that information to identify the variation in attitudes among the participants. This is a key stimulus to the discussion that follows, as the moderator tends to focus on those people who are at either end of the scale in order to identify why some were very positive and others negative about the idea.

Ranking—A process used in focus groups in which participants are asked to determine the relative value of a list of attributes or characteristics so that they can easily be discussed in the group. Normally, a moderator might ask the group to circle about 20% of the list they are provided to be indicative of the most important elements. Then, by reviewing the full list with the group and focusing only on the ones that are identified as most important, the moderator can obtain relatively easily a relative ranking of the various items that will be discussed.

Recommendations—The section of the final report that suggests the next action steps a client could take, based on the conclusions of the research.

Recruiter—see **Interviewer.**

Recruitment—The process of securing participants for focus groups.

Release form—The form that some clients and facilities ask participants to sign to release them from all responsibility for any consequences of the groups, especially when participants must taste food, alcohol, or tobacco products.

Rescreening—A brief interview conducted with potential participants when they arrive at a facility to ensure that they really qualify for the session. Rescreening normally uses some of the questions that were asked when the participants were originally recruited.

Respondent—see **Participant.**

Sample—The participants in a focus group as research subjects.

Screener—The questionnaire used to recruit participants. Most moderators review the screener before a session to become familiar with the participant types and to ensure that the recruitment has been correct.

Sentence completion—A moderation technique in which participants are asked to finish a sentence that has been started for them. The purpose of this technique is to enable participants to delve into certain areas that they may otherwise find difficult to discuss.

Significant influencer—An individual who does not have the final decision-making power in an organization but does have sufficient influence on those who do, so that he or she becomes a more important person to talk with than the ultimate decision maker. Normally, the significant influencer will be much more familiar with the topic area than the decision maker.

Sign-out sheet—A control document used by a facility to keep track of co-op payments to participants.

Specifications—The criteria for participants in a focus group, involving their demographic characteristics, product usage, product awareness, and so on.

Spreadsheets—Summary charts that are normally produced by the organization doing the recruiting for a focus group to show the most important information about each of the participants. They normally include the name and the answers given to the two to four most important questions used in the recruiting process.

Syndicated research—Research conducted on behalf of two or more clients, who share the costs.

Target consumers—The type of people who are to participate in a focus group. See **Specifications.**

Telephone group—A qualitative research methodology in which 7 to 10 people are connected in a telephone conference call and a trained moderator leads them through a discussion about a particular topic. Telephone groups are typically used with people who normally would not communicate with each other due to competitive conflicts but who will participate in an anonymous telephone discussion.

Triad—A qualitative research methodology in which a moderator works with three respondents. Some researchers maintain that the limited number of participants in a triad permits the moderator to get more information from them than is possible in a mini-group or full group.

Value added—The extra value a moderator brings to a client by virtue of his or her previous training or experience.

Variable personality association—A moderator technique in which photographs are selected for a particular focus group to secure participants' reactions to a particular topic that they represent. The "variable" aspect of this technique is that the photos are tailored to the group rather than *fixed*, as in the people board.

Verbatim—A transcript of the actual comments participants make in a focus group. Many moderators include verbatims in their final reports to support their interpretation of the findings.

Video focus groups—see **Global focus.**

Viewing room—see **Back room.**

Warm-up—The initial period of a focus group, when the moderator begins the group discussion. The intent of this 10- to 20-minute segment is to get the participants comfortable talking in the group, while at the same time gathering the most general information about the topic area to be covered in the groups.

Web site—A place on the World Wide Web where a company or an individual can store information for others to access. It is an excellent way to make information available about your service to others, who might find it via an Internet search or as a result of a direct inquiry to learn more about your company.

Write-down—The process of having participants write down their views on a topic during a focus group. Moderators use write-downs to get participants to commit to their own point of view before other participants can influence them.

INDEX

ABOUT THE AUTHOR

Thomas L. Greenbaum is President of Groups Plus, a focus group and consulting company in Wilton, Connecticut. In addition to writing and lecturing, he moderates more than 150 focus groups a year. He is currently an adjunct professor of marketing at the Leonard Stern School of Business (NYU), where he teaches a course in marketing research, with a heavy orientation toward focus group research.

Printed in the United States
33306LVS00005B/190-195